LOST NOTTINGHAM
IN COLOUR

IAN D. ROTHERHAM

AMBERLEY

First published 2015

Amberley Publishing
The Hill, Stroud, Gloucestershire, GL5 4EP
www.amberley-books.com

Copyright © Ian D. Rotherham, 2015

The right of Ian D. Rotherham to be identified as the
Author of this work has been asserted in accordance with
the Copyrights, Designs and Patents Act 1988.

ISBN 978 1 4456 5339 6 (print)
ISBN 978 1 4456 5340 2 (ebook)

British Library Cataloguing in Publication Data.
A catalogue record for this book is available from the
British Library.

Typesetting by Amberley Publishing.
Printed in Great Britain.

CONTENTS

ABOUT THE AUTHOR

Ian Rotherham is Professor of Environmental Geography and Reader in Tourism and Environmental Change at Sheffield Hallam University. An ecologist and environmental historian, he is a worldwide authority on landscape history and urban environments. He has researched and written about Sheffield for many years and has campaigned for its conservation, improvement, and its wider promotion. He has published over 400 papers, articles, books and book chapters, has a popular BBC Radio Sheffield phone-in, and writes for local and regional newspapers, particularly the *Sheffield Star*, the *Sheffield Telegraph*, and the *Yorkshire Post*. He has written a book on *The Lost Fens*, the great wetlands north, south and east of the Trent Valley, and a recent book for Amberley on Sherwood – *Sherwood Forest and the Dukeries* – *a companion to the land of Robin Hood*. Ian also wrote *Lost Sheffield in Colour* for Amberley in the same series as the current volume. *Lost York in Colour* will follow in 2016.

Ian is a Regional Tourism Ambassador for Sheffield and South Yorkshire, and is active in the conservation and promotion of Sherwood Forest and surrounding areas. He has worked on the concept for the proposed Sherwood Regional Park and on several major nature-reserve proposals for the Nottinghamshire Wildlife Trust. Ian lectures widely to local groups and works closely with bodies such as the Wildlife Trust, Natural England, English Heritage, the National Trust and the RSPB.

INTRODUCTION:
NOTTINGHAM, A REMARKABLE CITY

The town of Nottingham is the neatest town I have seen. It is built of stone and has delicate large and long streets much like London and the houses are lofty and well built. The Market Place is very broad – out of which run two very large streets.

Celia Fiennes, late 1600s.

Nottingham is a city known throughout the world because of its historic association with the famous Sherwood Forest, Robin Hood and the Sheriff (the first being appointed in 1449, somewhat too late for the King John connection!). It was also the home of several major industries, most notably Nottingham lace, bicycles, and Player's cigarettes. Today, the city is the vibrant county town of Nottinghamshire, boasting two major universities, world-class theatres, and two professional football clubs. The city also hosts the Nottinghamshire Cricket club at Trent Bridge.

The artery of this remarkable city is the River Trent, which runs west to east across the southern lowlands before windings its way to the great Humber Estuary and the North Sea. Along the watercourse, there are ancient meadows and pastures, plus today, great power stations and gravel-extraction sites. Some of the latter are now converted, at least in part, into amazingly rich and visitor-friendly nature reserves with the Nottinghamshire Wildlife Trust.

In the 1700s, traveller and writer Daniel Defoe described Nottingham, a settlement of just under 10,000 people, as one of the most pleasant, beautiful towns in all of England. By the late 1600s, salt-glaze stoneware was being manufactured in Nottingham, and in the following century the hosiery industry grew rapidly and lacemaking began. Throughout the 1800s, the hosiery industry grew and the town's reputation for lace made it famous, with a lacemaking machine introduced in 1809. New industries were emerging to confirm Nottingham's growing status, with John Player founding Player's cigarettes in 1877. By 1887, Frank Bowden was making bicycles in Raleigh Street. Naming his company after the road, by 1910 Raleigh produced 50,000 bicycles annually. On the back of such success, the town became a city in 1897. Nottingham is steeped in history, culture and heritage and this is a remarkable journey of discovery for visitors, but also for many residents too. Furthermore, the city is justifiably known for its excellent shopping facilities and abundant eateries and entertainments.

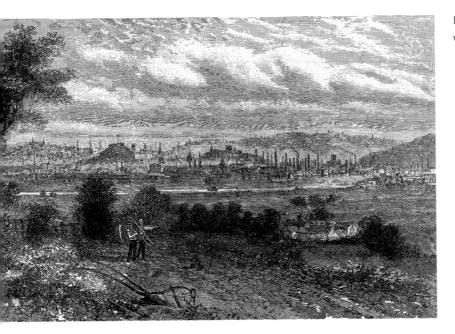

Distant view of Nottingham, in 1888, showing the floodplain and farmland with the expanding industrial town beyond.

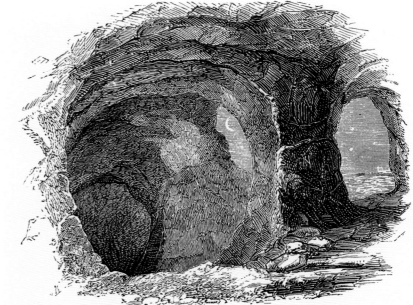

Mortimer's Hole under the castle, a place of mystery and intrigue..

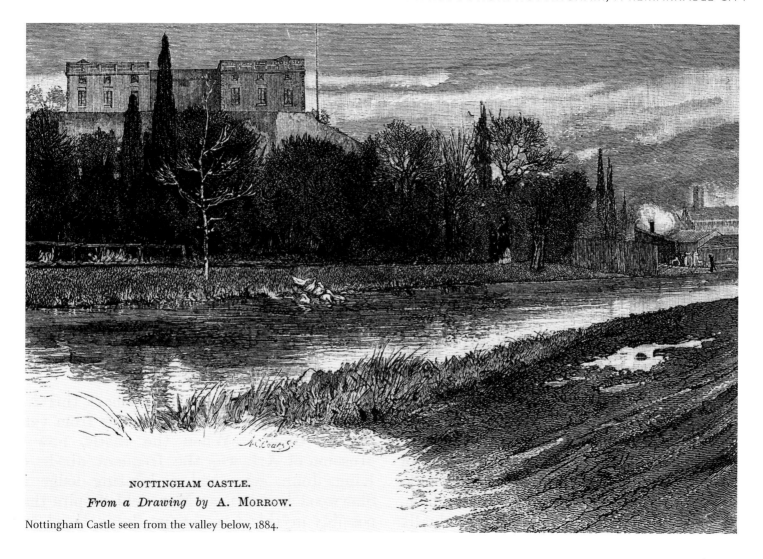

NOTTINGHAM CASTLE.

From a Drawing by A. MORROW.

Nottingham Castle seen from the valley below, 1884.

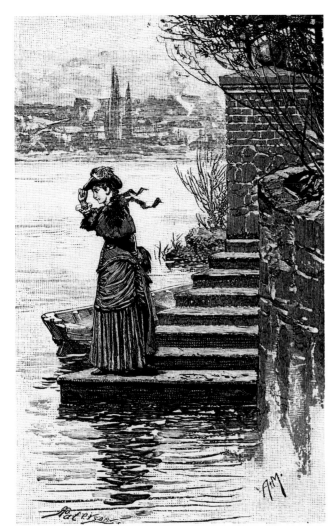

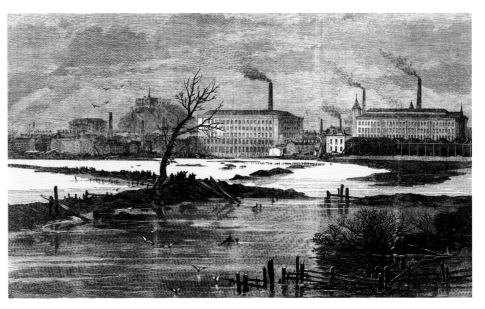

Above: Nottingham in flood, 1869. Proximity to a great river brings advantages but also many risks.

Left: On the Trent near Kimberley, 1884.

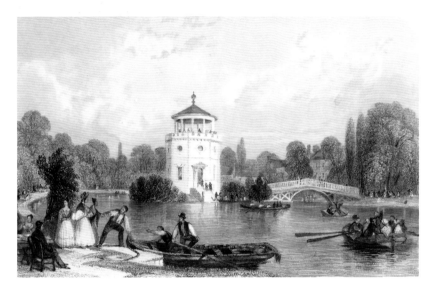

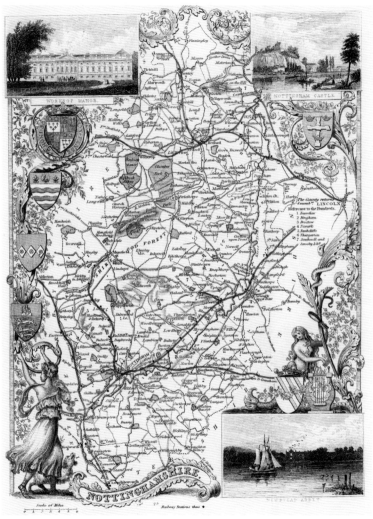

Above: Radford Folly, Nottingham, in the early 1800s, 'once a very popular pleasure resort and the rendezvous of the young men and maidens of Nottingham. It was in fact, a century ago, the local Vauxhall and its beauties'; by the late twentieth century a sad ruin remained and the lake had been infilled.

Right: Map of Nottinghamshire and the Dukeries.

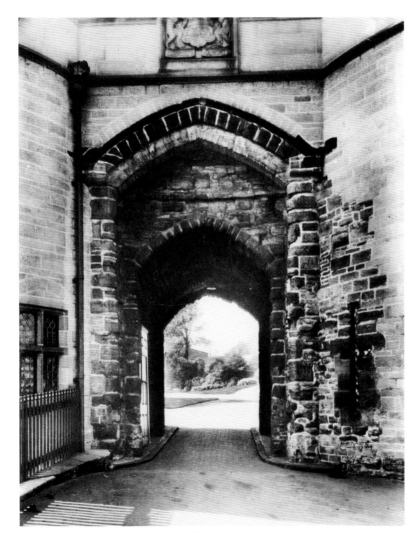

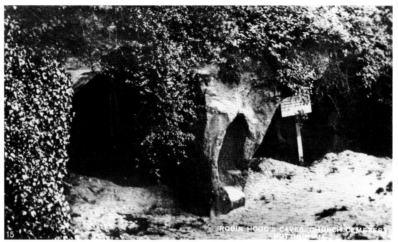

Above: Robin Hood's Caves and Church Cemetery, Nottingham, mid-1900s.

Left: The ancient gateway to Nottingham Castle in the mid-1900s.

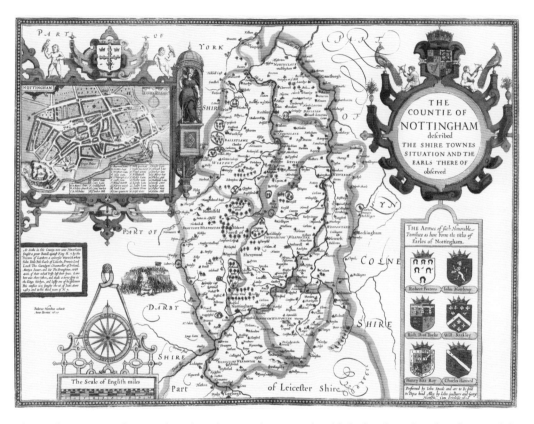

Above: The Countie of Nottingham by John Speed, 1610, and published in his atlas, the *Theatre of the Empire of Great Britain*, 1611.

Right: Victorian products from Nottingham – for personal hygiene and fresh breath.

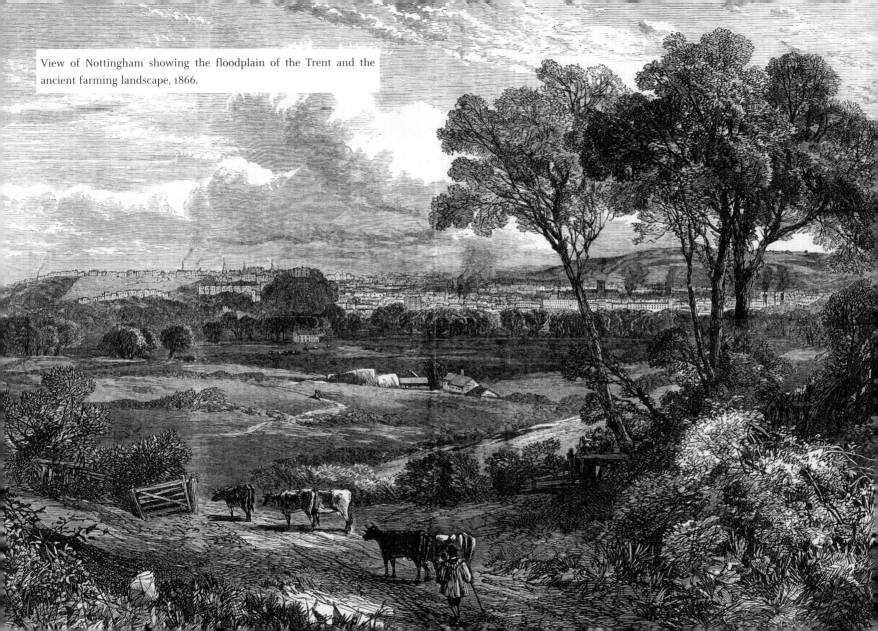

View of Nottingham showing the floodplain of the Trent and the ancient farming landscape, 1866.

1

THE TOWN CENTRE: OLD NOTTINGHAM, FROM MEDIEVAL TOWN TO MODERN CITY

Old Nottingham is on a low hill above the great floodplain of the River Trent. Modern redevelopment has removed much of the old city, but enough remains to provide insight into a remarkable past. The city has Anglo-Saxon beginnings, a Saxon settlement on high ground overlooking low-lying flood-land, but the area around the Trent was used by people long before then. Today's city really owes its origins to the Normans who built their first castle high on the rock escarpment and adjacent to the French Borough as the adjacent Saxon settlement became the English Borough; with a combined population of around 1,500 residents. Eventually the two boroughs became one, though the English site remained as the centre of the town's administration. This was some time after the 1066 conquest as William I sought to establish his authority in the north of England.

It gained its first Royal Charter in AD 1155 and soon had a weekly market and an annual fair. By the 1300s, it had around 3,000 people – for the time a big population. With a growing wool trade, Nottingham would be buzzing with craftsmen and traders such as tilers, goldsmiths, brewers, bakers, carpenters, shoemakers, blacksmiths, bridlesmiths, wheelwrights, fletchers and many more. The subsequent history of Nottingham, over maybe 500 to 600 years, was intimately linked to its castle and to national politics and power struggles leading up to the English Civil War in the 1600s.

In 1651, after the war, Parliament ordered that Nottingham Castle be demolished to avoid it becoming a Royalist stronghold. In 1674 the Duke of Newcastle bought the site. As the need for fortifications diminished and the desire for comfort and status grew, the castle was replaced by a grand ducal mansion for the fabulously wealthy Duke of Newcastle. The house was built there between 1674 and 1679. Around the streets spreading out from the mansion, still called the castle, into the town beyond, wealthy residents began to build fashionable houses and villas. Similarly, the Old Borough also became gentrified with large houses. However, as the urban areas became more industrialised during the 1800s, the wealthier locals moved outwards to more rural locations. As the gentry moved out, the industrial workers moved in, with the big houses becoming the homes and warehouses of the expanding hosiery industries. During the 1800s, the lacemaking industry overtook hosiery in importance and as houses soon became inadequate for their new purposes, many were demolished and replaced by purpose-built fine warehouses and factories. During the early twentieth century the lace industry declined and the area, known since the mid-1800s as The Lace Market, was left very rundown. Part of Nottingham's resurgence in the latter part of the twentieth century included the renovation of this area.

History perhaps suggests that the dukes might have been wise to keep their defensive castle because the political situation in the 1830s led to the great unpopularity of the then duke. The upshot was that the mansion was ransacked and burnt by the mob in 1831. Subsequent restoration saw the building reopened as a museum and art gallery in 1878, the ceremony attended by the Prince and Princess of Wales in July of that year. A visit to the castle is a must for those new to the city, and from its lofty perch the site offers great views across much of the modern-day landscape.

Below the castle and along the southern side of the park are the remarkable old caves of which Nottingham is famous. Sometimes described as chapels, Papist holes, and hermit dwellings, the house built above the caves by John Leavers was called The Hermitage. It is suggested that the Hermitage Caves along Castle Boulevard were most likely to have been used as storerooms. Fish from the River Leen, a tributary of the Trent, were cleaned here for use in the castle. Small holes in the rocks were probably used as dovecotes, again to provide winter food for the castle. Some of the caves were later incorporated into the gardens of new houses and people used them for storerooms or event summerhouses. Sadly, many were lost under industrial development during the 1800s and 1900s. Place names and street names reflect past usage, with Fishponds Drive, Fishpond Garden, The Ropewalk and more.

Brewhouse Yard formerly held the brewhouses to the castle, an important consideration for an important settlement, and names or places came and went throughout history and needs changed and locations recycled. Interestingly, the Brewhouse Yard area was classed as a small township outside the administration of Nottingham Town, thus residents were beyond the reach of the local laws. The result was that this small community attracted rogues and criminals who were outside the town's laws and legal enforcement. This situation ended with the Borough Extension Act of 1877.

Other problems with Nottingham's growth were things like the stench, filth and pollution associated with the canal and its wharfs. By the 1890s, the canal was the responsibility of the Great Northern Railway when the solicitors for the Duke of Newcastle wrote to them complaining that it was nothing more than an open sewer. However, the end was close for this industrial site as a new lower road was needed to meet Gregory Boulevard, and the wharfs were filled and the canal diverted. By 1884, Castle Boulevard was constructed and opened. The newly opened Castle Boulevard allowed traffic to have speedier access to the Midland railway station, though the canal still carried heavy, bulk freight. There was a transhipment warehouse which allowed the exchange of goods between the wider riverboats of the Trent, and the narrower barges of the canal. The transfer of goods took place in a tunnel underneath the building, which more recently has housed the canal museum.

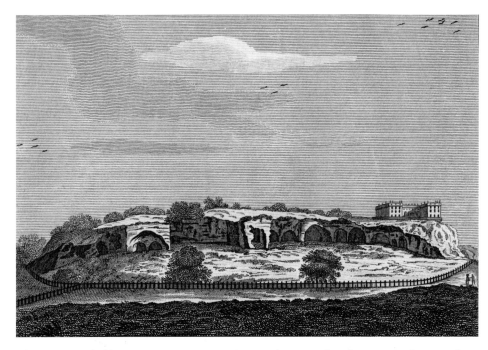

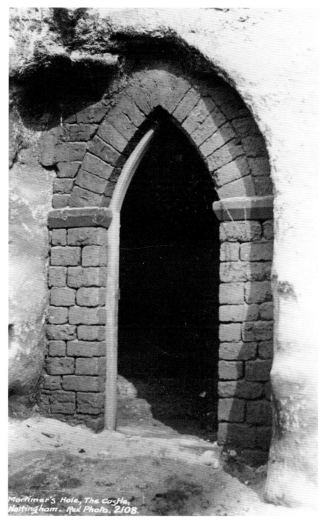

Above: A remarkable ancient ruin in Nottingham Park, pictured in the 1700s with Nottingham Castle in the distance. These ancient cave dwellings in the soft sandstone have acquired practical uses of the centuries, along with both history and mythology.

Right: Entrance to Mortimer's Hole, Nottingham Castle, in the mid-1900s. This is the most famous of all the entrances.

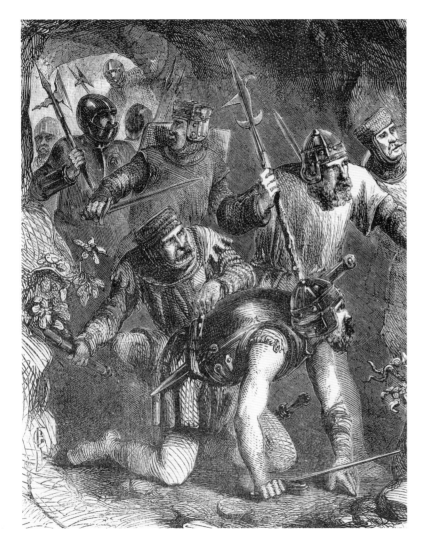

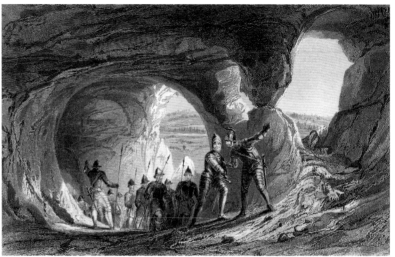

Above: Mortimer's Hole under Nottingham Castle.

Left: In the secret tunnel beneath the castle during the reign of Edward III.

Nottingham Castle around the early 1900s with the ancient gateway giving some indication of the solidarity of the fortifications.

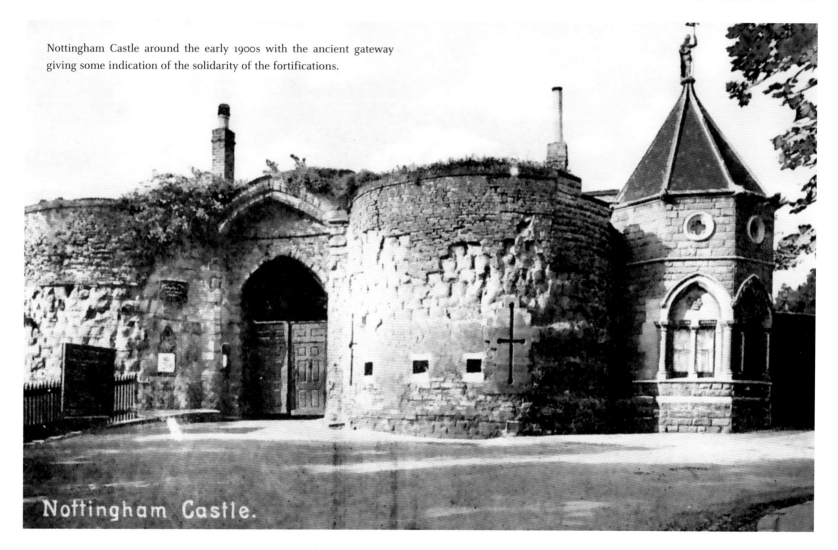

Nottingham Castle.

Nottingham Castle entrance, *c.* 1908, now a local cultural site rather than a defensive one.

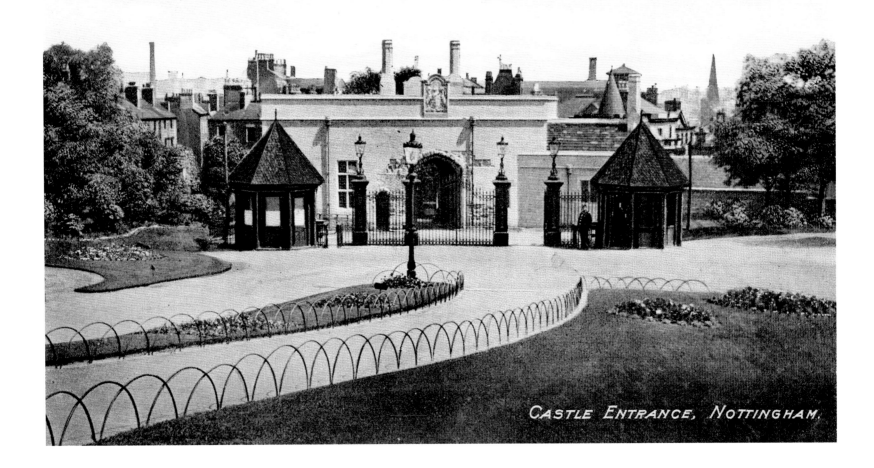

CASTLE ENTRANCE, NOTTINGHAM.

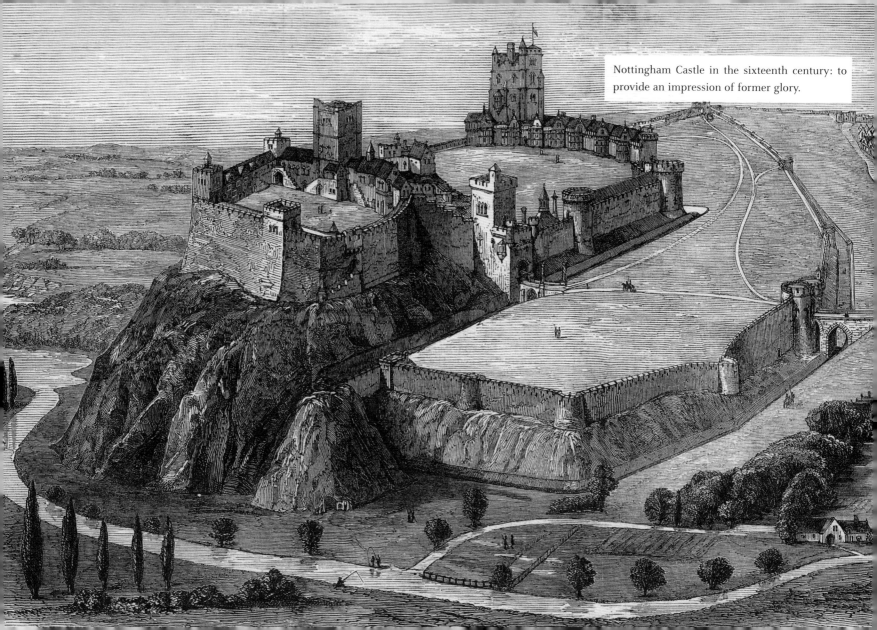

Nottingham Castle in the sixteenth century: to provide an impression of former glory.

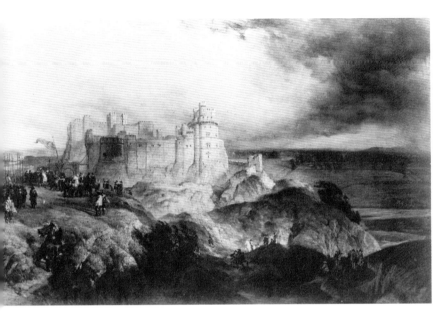

Nottingham Castle in the seventeenth century, standing proud and imposing on the high rocky escarpment.

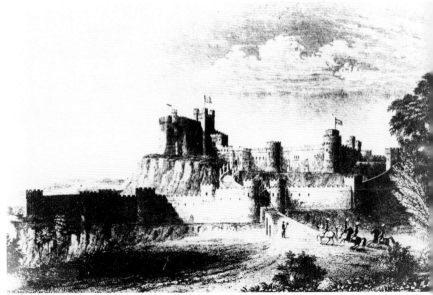

Nottingham Castle in the sixteenth century, showing the outer defensive wall.

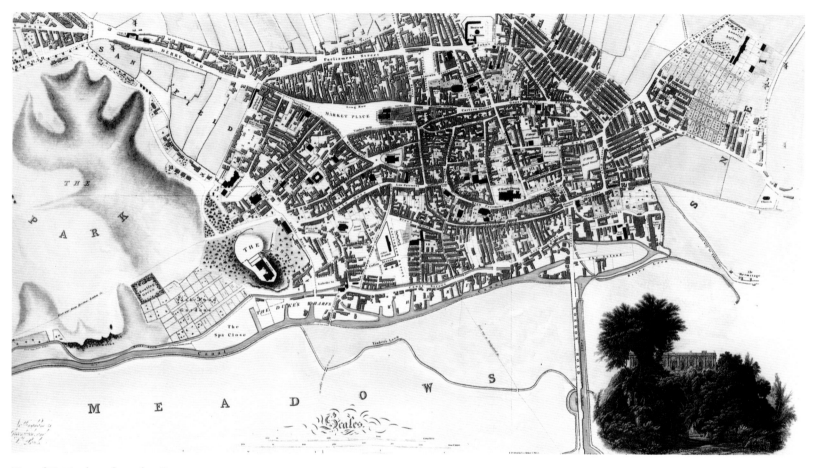

Map of Nottingham from the 1820s.

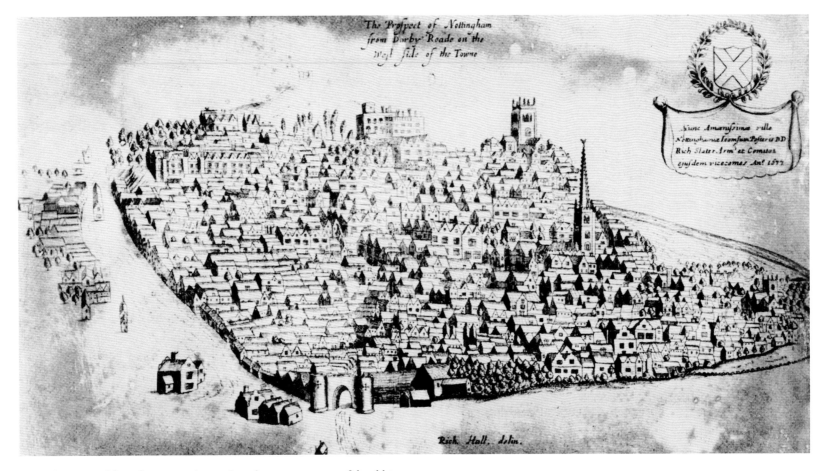

The 'Prospect of Nottingham
from Darby Roade on the
West side of the Towne

Nunc Amanissima ville
Nottinghamia Icomsum Posteris DD
Rich Slater Arm' et Comstos
ejusdem vicecomes An.o 1677

Rich Hall, delin.

Nottingham viewed from the west, *c.* 1677, to show the compact nature of the old town.

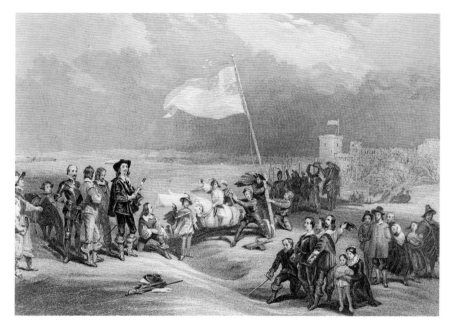

Above: Raising the Royal Standard at Nottingham in the 1640s in the midst of civil war that would spell the end of the old castle.

Right: Statue of Robin Hood at Nottingham Castle by James Woodford was erected in 1952.

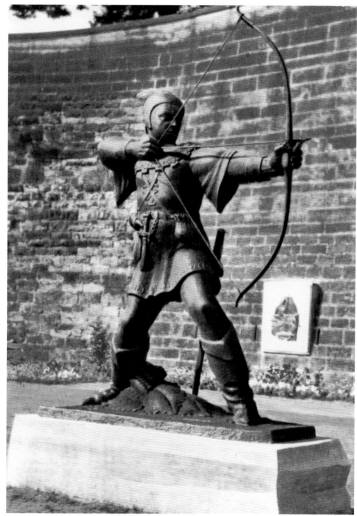

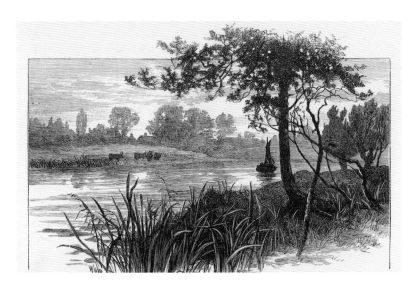

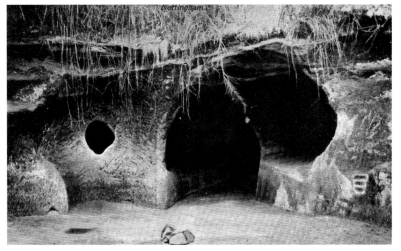

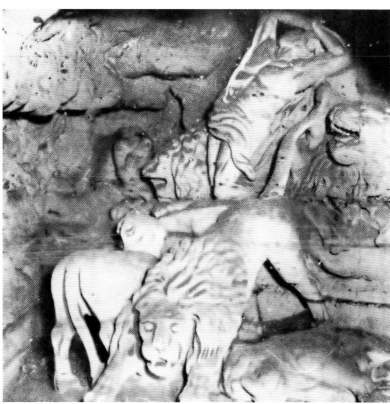

Above left: River Trent in the 1800s.

Above right: Rock carvings in a cave on the Ropewalk, pictured in the 1920s.

Below left: Robin Hood's Cave, Nottingham, 1904.

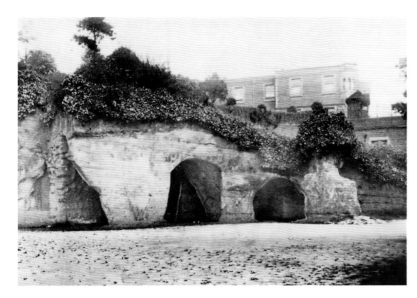

Above: Rock Holes, The Hermitage, Castle Boulevard, pictured in the 1920s.

Right: Shire Hall Dungeons, the High Pavement, which was the county gaol for Nottinghamshire and Derbyshire and, for a time, part of the smallest civil parish in England.

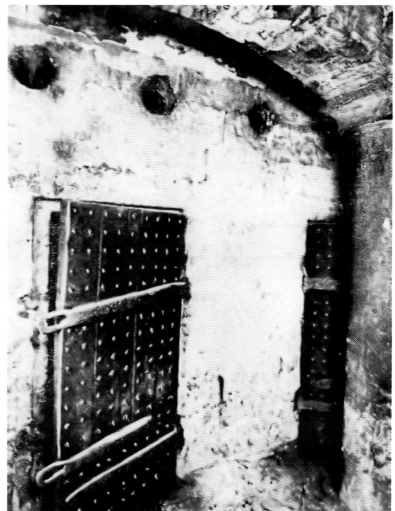

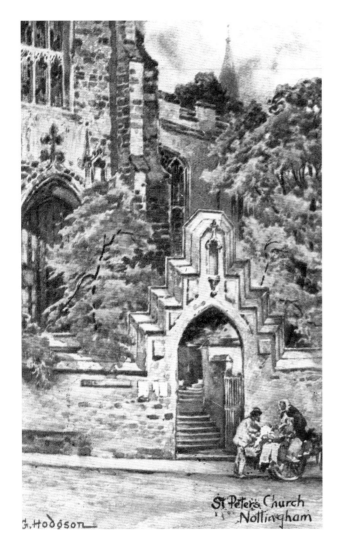

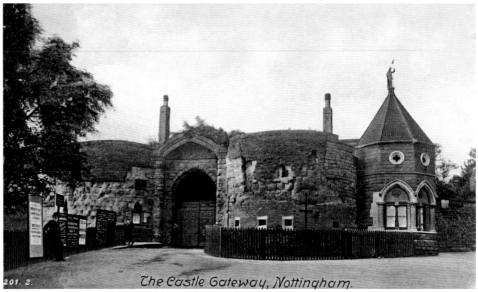

Above: The Castle Gateway Nottingham, pictured around 1909.

Left: St Peter's church, 1903.

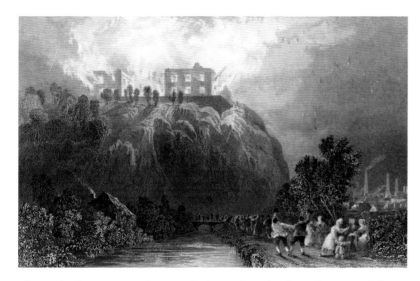

Above: The fire at Nottingham Castle, burnt down by the mob in 1831, left as a ruin, and later rebuilt as the museum.

Right: The Old Gate of Nottingham Castle, pictured in 1866.

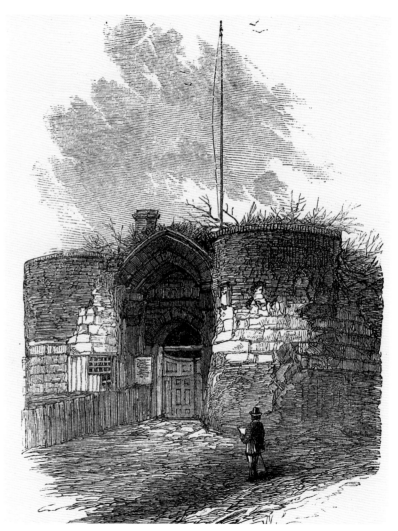

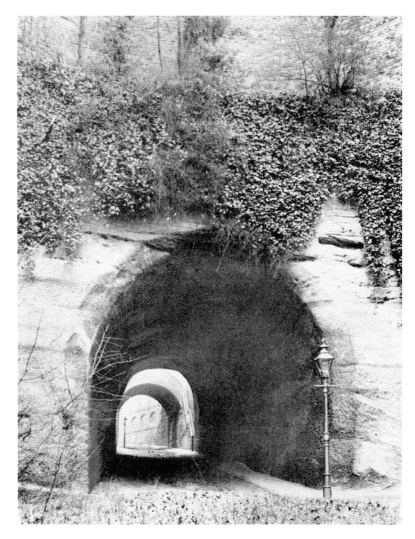

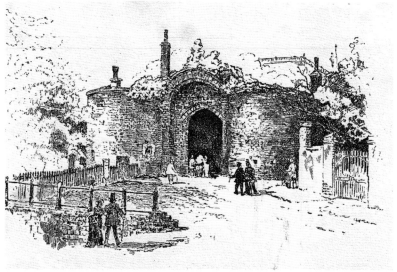

Above: The Old Gateway, Nottingham Castle, in 1888 with visitors walking up the road to the entrance.

Left: The Park Tunnel in Nottingham Castle Park, photographed in the 1920s.

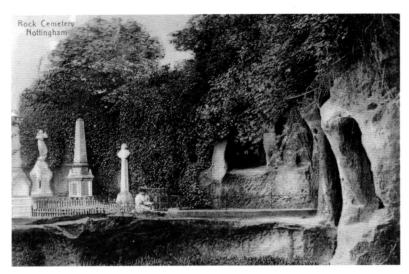

Above: The Rock Cemetery, Nottingham, *c.* 1905.

Right: The remaining part of the old front of Thirland Hall in Grindlesmithygate Nottingham, the possession of His Grace the Duke of Newcastle, in 1750.

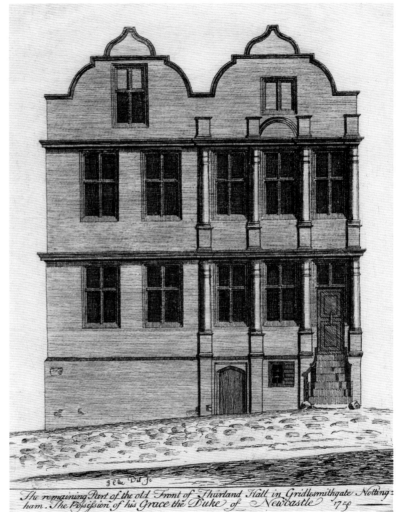

The remaining Part of the old Front of Thirland Hall in Gridlesmithgate Nottingham. The Possession of his Grace the Duke of Newcastle 1750

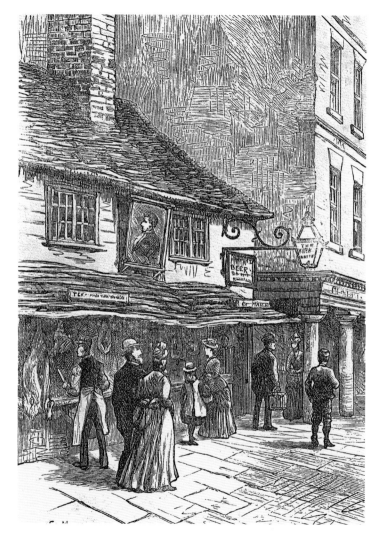

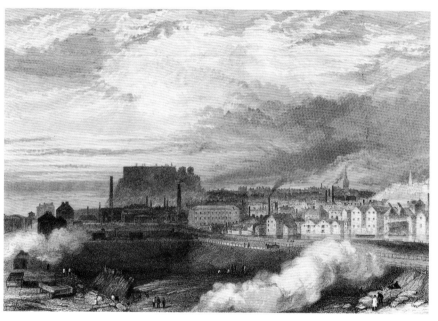

Above: A rather sombre view of Nottingham and the castle in the 1800s.

Left: The birthplace of Kirke White, talented Nottingham poet, pictured in 1888.

2

INDUSTRY & COMMERCE: NOTTINGHAM'S EMERGENCE WITH INDUSTRY & URBAN SETTLEMENT

From an important medieval beginning, Nottingham grew rapidly in the nineteenth and twentieth centuries to become a centre for trade, commerce and industry. By 1801, the town had a population of over 28,000 people – at that time a significant centre and growing rapidly. Key industries were hosiery, then lace, bicycles with Raleigh and others, cigarettes with Player's, and of course Boots PLC. Many of the factories that powered the Industrial Revolution here have long-since gone. Some are now restored to new functions and others have been cleared, the dereliction and pollution removed, and the sites recycled for twenty-first – century uses. Like a phoenix rising from the ashes, a new vibrant city has emerged.

As the economic hub of the city expanded, so too did the housing estates. Some became desirable, green, suburbs and others emerged as vast, sprawling, high-density slums. The latter have gone, but even the modern estates can be soulless places unless they retain a core of old settlements and older landscapes to give a sense of place and to touch the past identity.

Alan Sillitoe captured the social context and even desperation of working-class life in mid-twentieth-century Nottingham, in his highly acclaimed 1958 book *Saturday Night and Sunday Morning*. The book became a global phenomenon with the release of the 1960 film directed by Karel Reisz, produced by Tony Richardson, and starring Albert Finney. Much, but not all, of the filming was on location in Nottingham; some scenes filmed in London were made up to look like Nottingham. As a youngster, Sillitoe lived mostly in Radford, in 2008 describing it to James Walker as 'very good really. It was a jungle. I don't mean a terrible jungle, but a benign jungle where we knew every twist and turn and double alley'. Sillitoe goes on: 'We all felt perfectly safe as kids and it was a good place to grow up actually. I had a good education at Radford Boulevard. They taught me to read, taught me to write, they gave me an interest in history and geography, and that's all I needed.'

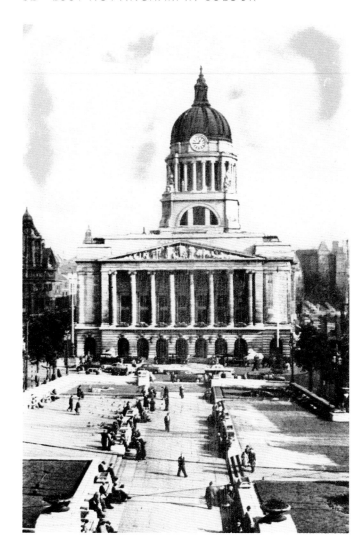

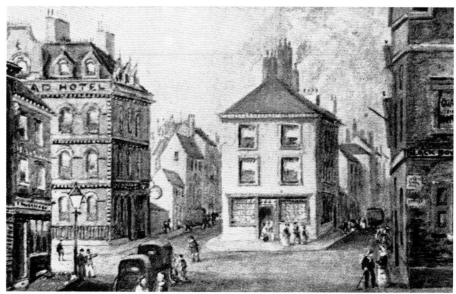

Above: Bunkers Hill and Parliament Row in 1880.

Left: Council House Square in the 1950s, as part of the modernisation of a now grand city.

HULMES HIGH-CLASS ❧

Artificial Teeth Depot,

LORD'S CHAMBERS, 84, UPPER PARLIAMENT ST., NOTTINGHAM.

Messrs. Hulmes guarantee their Teeth to be made from the best materials, and to be perfectly adapted on all known methods by the most skilled in the profession.

Speciality—20/- Sets fit for Royalty.

Special terms to Domestics.   Arrangements for easy payments when required.

TEETH ON GOLD, PLATINA, &c., AT HALF USUAL RATES.

Note the Address: **84 UPPER PARLIAMENT ST.**

1895

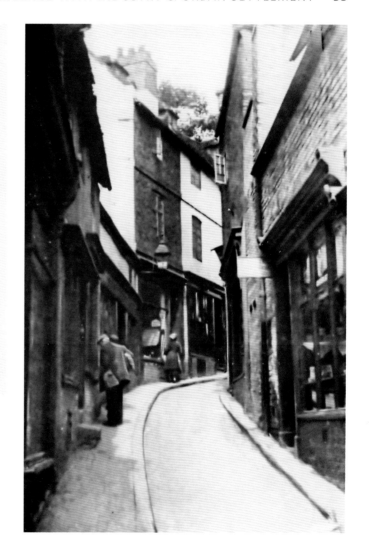

Above: Denture advert in the 1890s.

Right: Narrow and winding Drury Hill, from Low Pavement to Sussex Street in the 1920s.

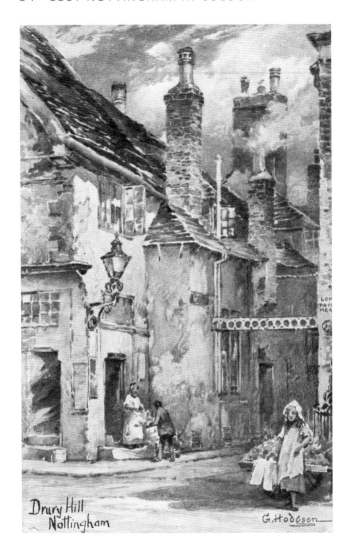

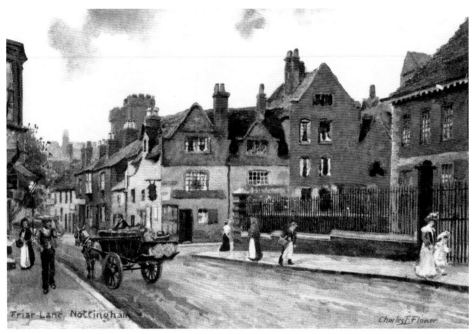

Above: Friar Lane in the early 1900s, a wider and more modern thoroughfare.

Left: Drury Hill, Nottingham in the 1800s, a view of typical urban poverty in Victorian England.

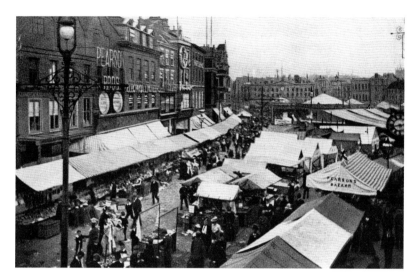

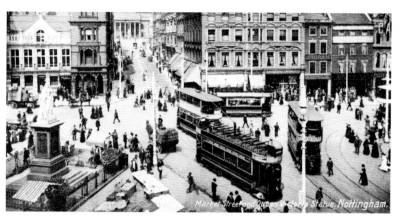

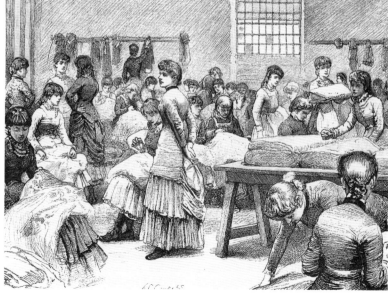

Above left: Long Row, Nottingham during the Goose Fair in the early 1900s.

Above right: The hustle and bustle of Market Street and Queen Victoria Statue, 1914.

Below right: One of the mainstays of local employment – mending lace curtains, 1884.

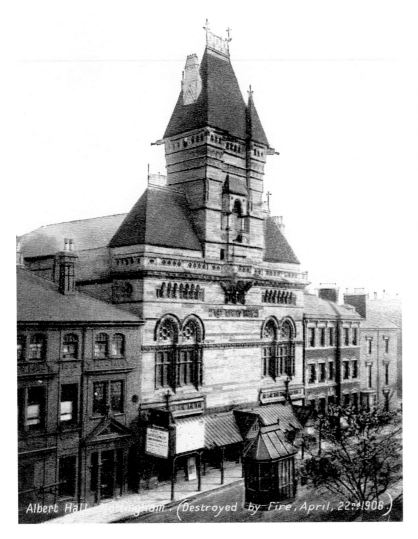

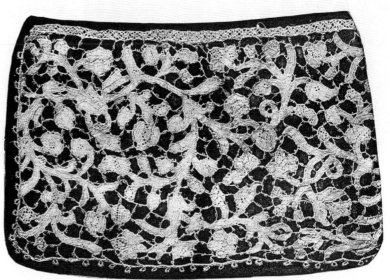

Above: Nottingham Lace specimen of Italian Point-lace, 1884.

Left: Nottingham Albert Hall, destroyed by fire on 22 April 1908.

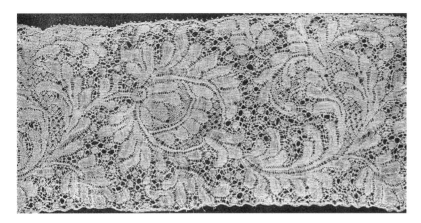

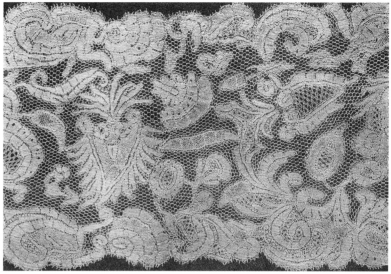

Above left: Nottingham Lace specimen of Old Flanders Pillow-lace, 1884.

Above right: Nottingham Lace specimen of Point D'Angleterre, 1884.

Below right: Nottingham Lace specimen of True Point – Point d'Alencon, 1884.

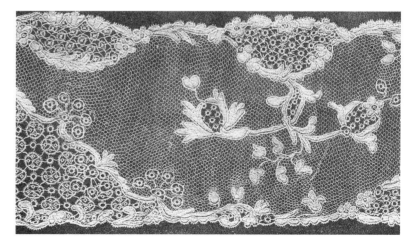

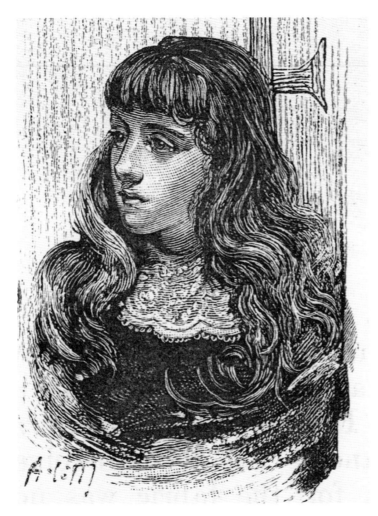

Nottingham lacemaking girl, 1884.

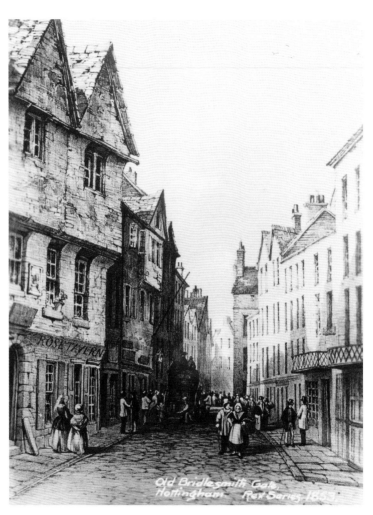

Old Bridlesmith Gate around 1853.

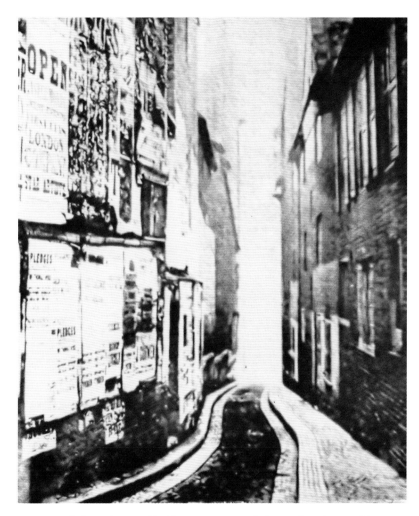

Narrow and almost impassable, Sheep Lane towards the Market Place in 1865.

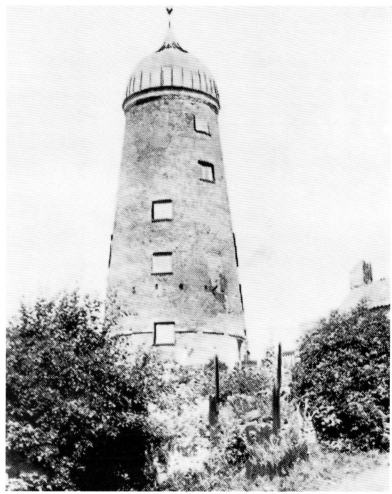

Sneinton Mill – the last windmill in Nottingham, photographed in the 1920s.

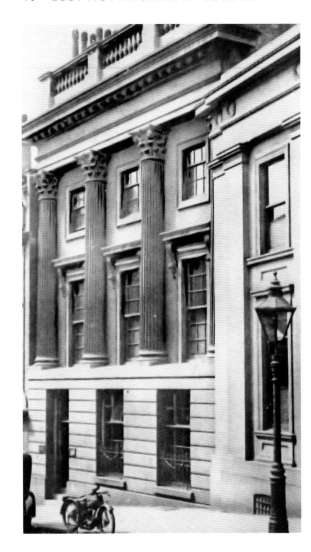

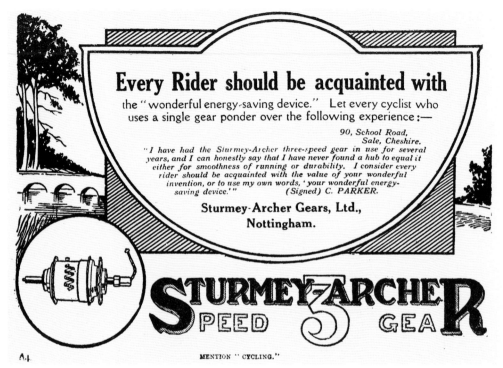

Above: Nottingham became synonymous with cycling and this Sturmey-Archer advert, for 1917, is a reminder of a fine manufacturer of bicycle gears.

Left: A symbol of economic and civic pride, the Old Assembly Rooms, No. 7 Low Pavement, in the 1920s.

The Old Guildhall, 1888.

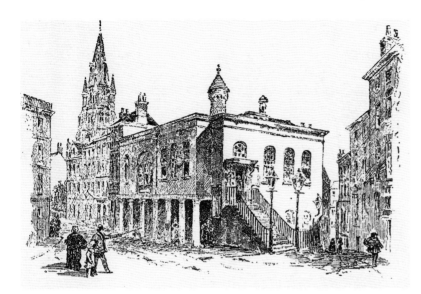

View of early industrial Nottingham.

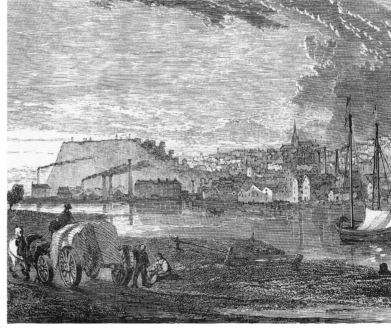

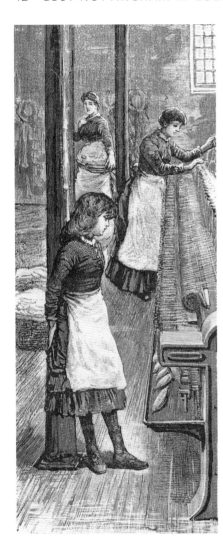

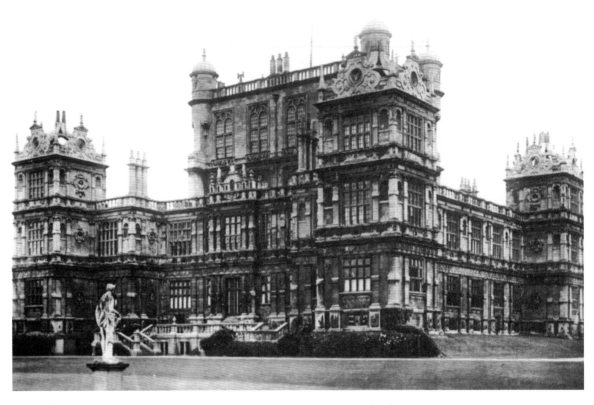

Above: Wollaton Hall is one the largest sixteenth-century mansions in England.

Left: Victorian employment with a child winding the cotton yarn, 1884.

3

AROUND NOTTINGHAM: A TOWN OF GREAT HOUSES & ESTATES

Sherwood and the Dukeries now lie to the north of Nottingham, although the city was once inside the forest boundary. The Dukeries name, used since the eighteenth century and applied to a large tract of Nottinghamshire, derived from the presence of five grand ducal estates. Indeed, much of the surviving Sherwood Forest remains because it was encapsulated within the aristocratic domains. The five great estates today are Welbeck, Clumber, Thoresby, Workshop Manor, and Rufford, though the latter was never actually ducal. Along with these are smaller houses and halls, and sites such as Nottingham Castle and Wollaton Hall to the south, and Bolsover Castle and Hardwick Hall to the west.

The fourth Duke of Newcastle-under-Lyme was the incumbent of the grand Clumber Park. He was apparently highly regarded, and for the times a humane man, but became the target of severe animosity from radical groups. A high Tory, he was against social and political change, especially the Reform Bill, and consequently was viewed as a manifestation of Tory reaction and deeply embedded social privilege. Because of his high profile and entrenched views, in October 1832 an irate mob attacked his Nottingham house, Nottingham Castle. It was burnt to the ground. In London, rioters stoned the duke's house in Portman Square, although by the time they arrived it had been fortified sufficiently to more or less protect it. As a consequence, the duke was given a large sum of money as compensation for the damage, though this did not go toward the restoration of the mansion. Having been considered as the site for a prison, the building was reopened in the 1870s as a museum and art gallery overlooking what became the Park Estate.

The Nottingham area has many fine halls houses and estates, and Newstead Abbey is one of the most spectacular. Sold by Charles Fraser to philanthropist Sir Julien Cahn, Newstead Abbey and a museum of Byron memorabilia are today owned by Nottingham City Council. Cahn presented the house to Nottingham Corporation in 1931. Located between Nottingham and Mansfield, the house and the estate have the long, often tortuous and frequently romantic history as found with many Sherwood locales. The link to the poet Lord Byron makes Newstead, and indeed Nottingham, a place of global literary significance.

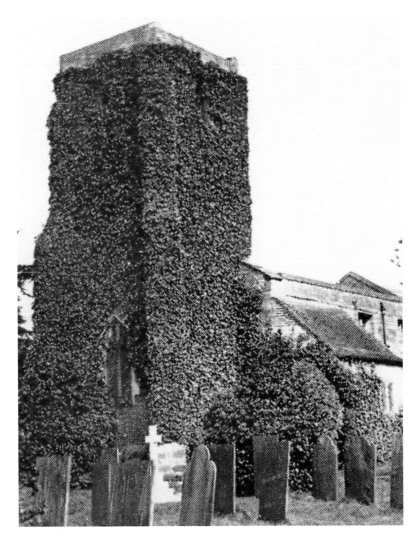

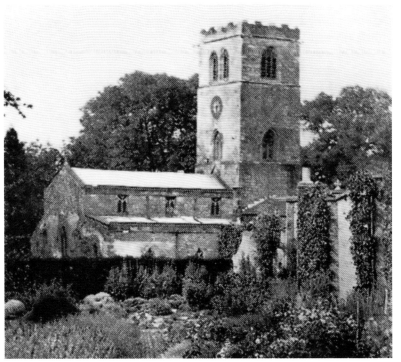

Above: a reminder of rural past – Clifton church, photographed in the 1920s.

Left: Edwalton church, pictured in the 1920s.

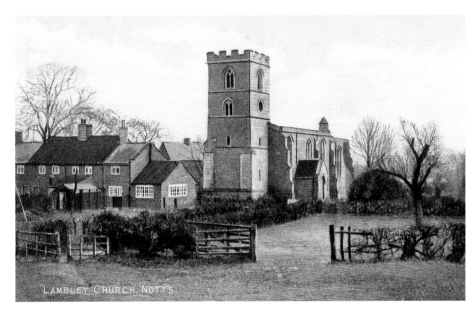

Above: Lambley church in the eastern rural suburbs beyond Arnold in the early 1900s.

Right: Market Cross and Maypole at rural Linby just north of Hucknall in the early 1900s.

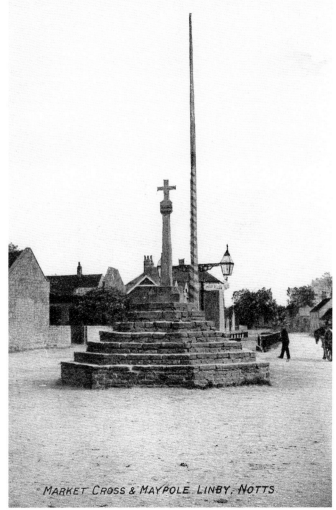

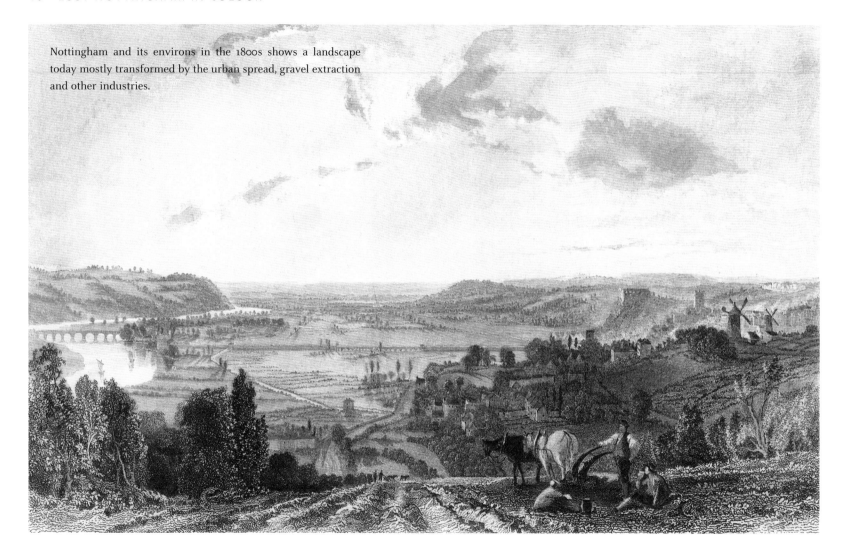

Nottingham and its environs in the 1800s shows a landscape today mostly transformed by the urban spread, gravel extraction and other industries.

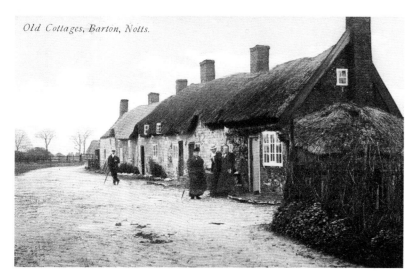

Old Cottages, Barton, Notts.

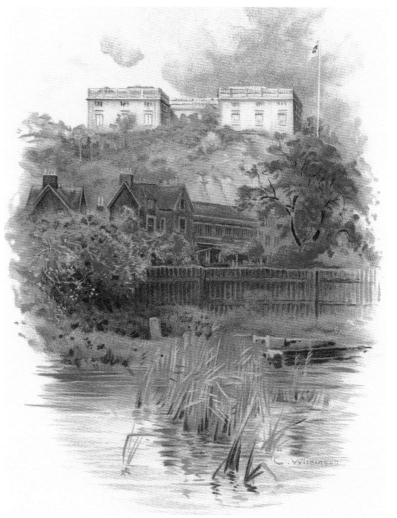

Above: Old cottages at Barton on the south-west fringes of Nottingham in 1905.

Right: Nottingham Castle in the 1800s, an imposing but modern building.

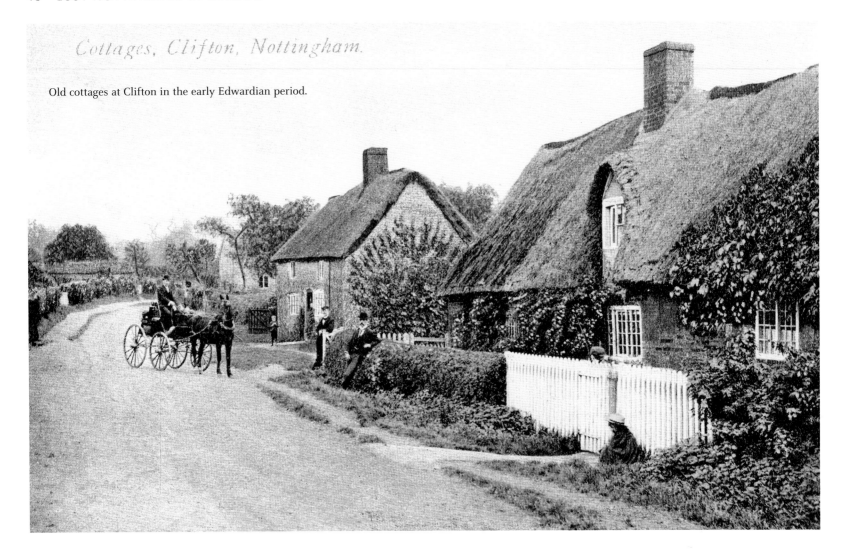

Old cottages at Clifton in the early Edwardian period.

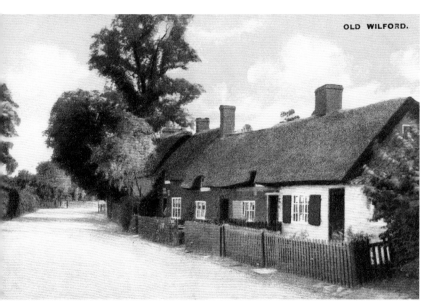

Old cottages at Wilford Nottingham in around 1904.

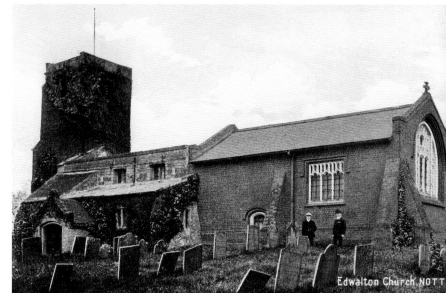

Old Edwalton church in the rural fringe suburb of Edwalton, south of the river, in around 1907.

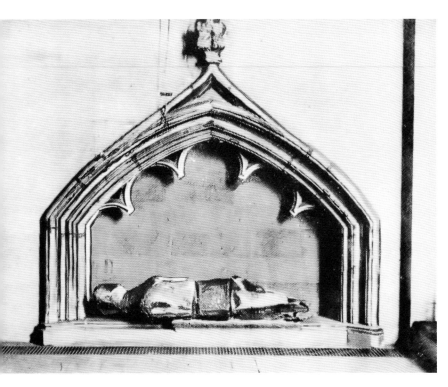

The Stone Man, West Bridgford church dating, from the reign of Edward I and once taken for use as a roadside boundary marker.

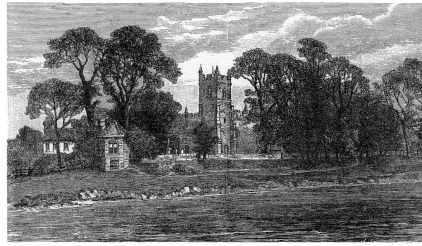

Wilford church, Nottingham, 1888.

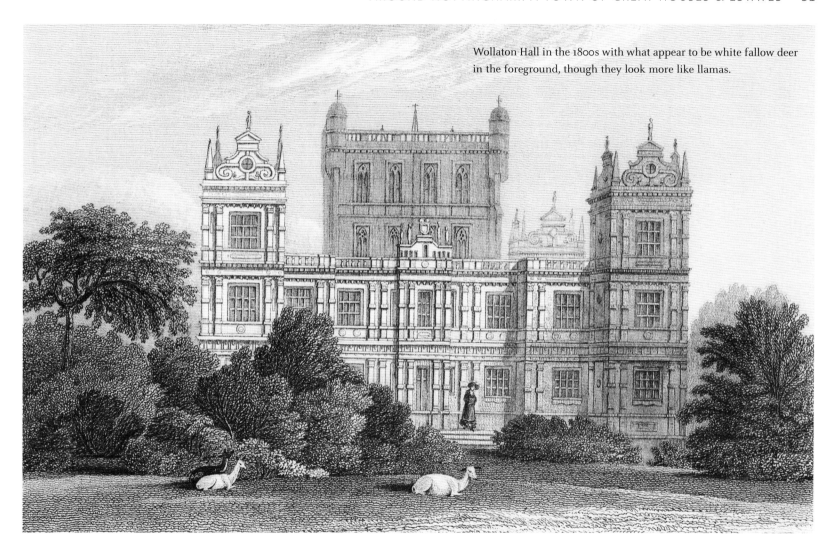

Wollaton Hall in the 1800s with what appear to be white fallow deer in the foreground, though they look more like llamas.

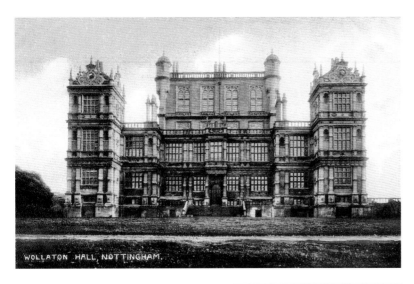

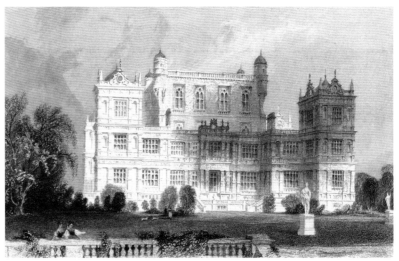

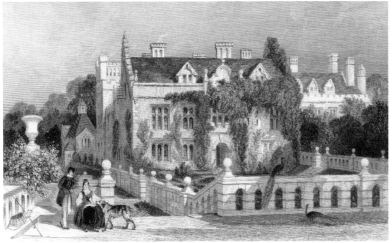

Above left: Wollaton Hall in around 1906 with its dramatic and imposing frontage.

Above right: Wollaton Hall in the early 1800s with the ladies of the house enjoying the pleasure gardens.

Below left: Newstead Abbey, intimately tied to Nottingham and the poet Lord Byron.

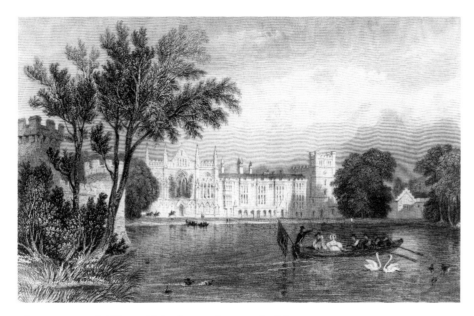

Above: Newstead Abbey with its famous boat on the lake.

Right: Nottingham has long been a centre for tourism and leisure in association with Sherwood Forest – as seen here in 'Rambles in Nottinghamshire and the Dukeries'.

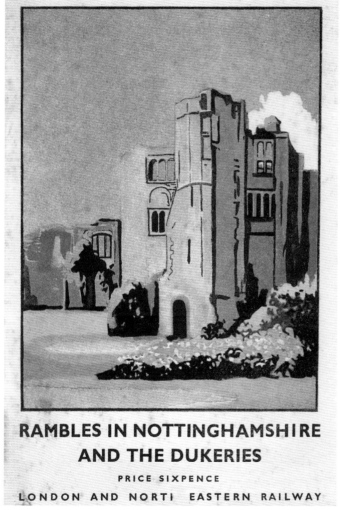

RAMBLES IN NOTTINGHAMSHIRE
AND THE DUKERIES

PRICE SIXPENCE

LONDON AND NORTI EASTERN RAILWAY

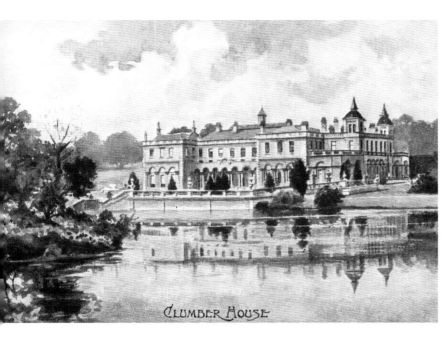

Clumber House, early 1900s, prior to demolition in the 1930s.

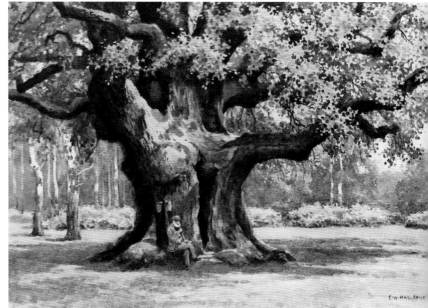

Perhaps the most iconic tree in the world, the Major Oak in Sherwood Forest.

4

A CITY OF A RIVER & A ROYAL FOREST

Nottingham emerged in the early medieval period as a strategic crossing point on the River Trent, the river being a natural trading waterway for commerce down to the Humber Estuary and from there to Europe. The city was sufficiently far north for royal visits and to be a stronghold of power in the Midlands, but it was not so far as to be isolated from the political hub of London. This was an important consideration in medieval England often torn apart by civil strife and unrest. Proximity to Sherwood Forest provided opportunities for royal sport, for meetings with foreign dignitaries, and an escape from the commotion of London. Though much reduced in extent today, in the medieval times much of modern Nottingham was within the boundaries of the royal forest.

The ancient forest was mostly open oak and birch heath apart from two main areas between Nottingham and Mansfield, and north from Edwinstowe to Ollerton. In these was more dense woodland, with both sessile and English oaks. The name Sherwood is not clear though wood is from 'wudu', the Old English for extensively wooded landscape. 'Sher' may be from 'shire', i.e. the county's wood, or 'bright' or 'famous'. Sherwood as the 'Shire-Wood' seems reasonable. The forest boundaries seem to have varied considerably over time, and in 1218 Henry III despatched a jury of knights and freemen to ride the perimeter of the royal forest. They went as far as Southwell and Laxton in the south-east, and to the outskirts of Chesterfield in the north-west.

If Sherwood provided a hub for the city, the River Trent provided its artery. Waterborne transport would allow movement of materials into and out of Nottingham, and especially of manufactured goods downstream and export to the European markets. Today, much cleaner than even a few decades ago, the Trent and its nature reserves is a haven for fish such as trout, for mammals like otters, roe deer and water voles, and for diverse birdlife including cormorants, kingfishers, egrets, herons and other water birds.

As the city expanded, until the latter half of the nineteenth century, the marketplace was the main focus of commercial activity. Indeed, the built areas of the town spread only a little way around it. Nottingham became a city in 1897 and began to expand away from this core, for around 5 miles to the north, and around 1 mile to the south, with the marketplace no longer the geographic centre. Many buses run into the centre and the former market area is now an open space with flower beds and fountains and a formal way up to the city's council house.

Supplementing trade along the Trent, the opening of the Nottingham Canal in 1796 connected the town directly with the industrial centres inland, especially the Derbyshire coalfields towns, and indirectly to the country's ports too. The impact of the canal was short-lived as in less than a century it was displaced by the railways, the Great Northern Railway Bridge crossing the river upstream at Ratcliffe-on-Trent. One of the main trading areas was below Castle Rock where at Gordon's Wharf, Park Wharf, or Duke's Wharf coal barges and other vessels plied their trade. Barges might be repaired or even built in the boatyards around the wharfs.

Meanwhile, along the River Trent there was an increasing need to control the floodwaters, and by the early 1900s a new embankment was constructed with a footpath, Lovers' Walk, on the south bank. County Hall is located nearby.

From around 1880 to 1910, the Trent enjoyed something of a golden age in terms of recreation and leisure. As well as commercial river traffic there were rowing boats, pleasure steamers and even houseboats. From Colwick ran two steamers, the *Sunbeam* and the *Queen,* with a trip in around 1888 costing 2*d* on the open end of the boat and 3*d* on the upper deck. At Colwick Park there was a band, dancing, pleasure gardens with food and drink, and even a menagerie. Demand was such that by 1900 there was need for a third steamer, this time named *Empress*. She was even more impressive than the other two with a music room and a baby grand piano. The service was good, with boats leaving Trent Bridge every twenty minutes from 2.00 p.m. until 9.40 p.m., and the last return from Colwick was at 10.15 p.m. A remarkable twist in the tale is that the *Empress* ended her days as one of the flotilla of little boats that crossed the English Channel to rescue troops from Dunkirk in 1940. She was sunk on her second crossing.

Opened to traffic in March 1958 to take pressure off the Trent Bridge, the Clifton Bridge spans the River Trent, carrying the A52 road to the west of the city.

Castle Rock, Nottingham, in around 1912.

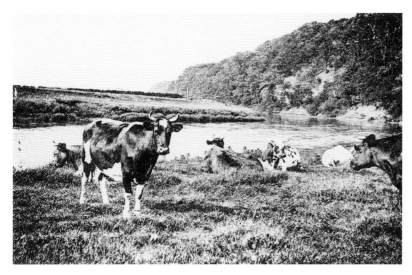

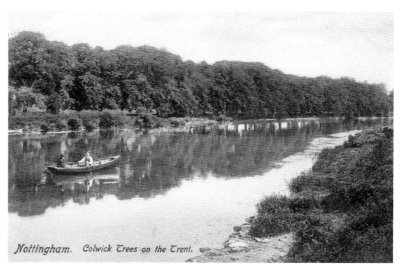

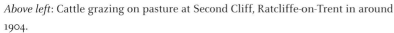

Above left: Cattle grazing on pasture at Second Cliff, Ratcliffe-on-Trent in around 1904.

Above right: Colwick Trees on the Trent at Nottingham, sent as a Christmas card in 1904.

Below right: Downstream of Nottingham, the Trent is famous for its tidal bore – the Aegir shown here in the early 1900s.

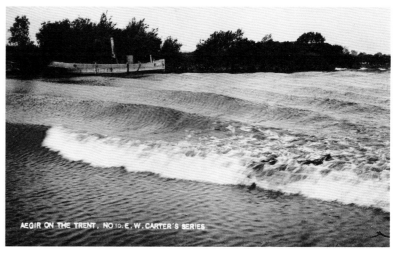

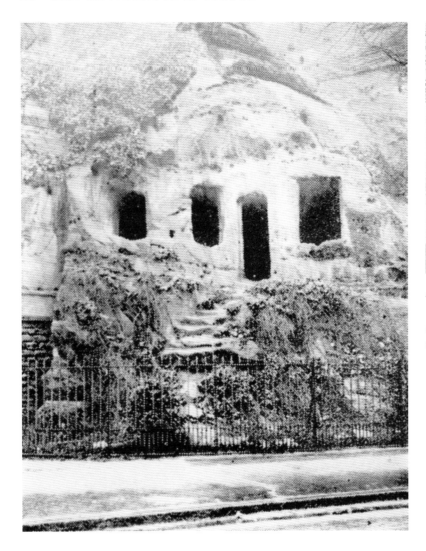

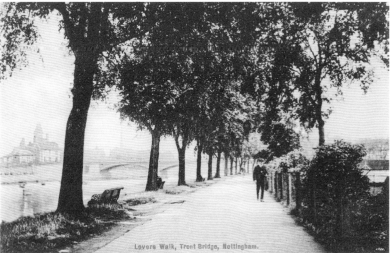

Above: Lovers Walk, Trent Bridge, Nottingham in around 1911.

Left: Houses in the Castle Rock, pictured in the 1920s with obvious windows and doorway.

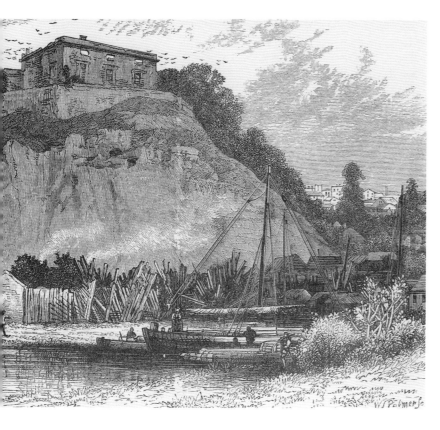

A fine view of an increasingly canalised River Trent, Nottingham mid-1900s.

Nottingham Castle, again in the 1800s, with the industrial waterway in the foreground.

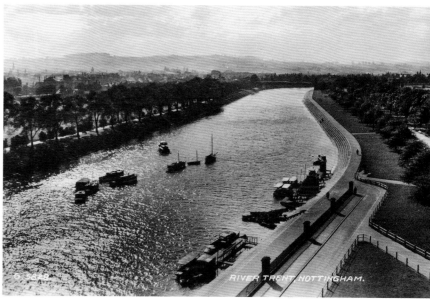

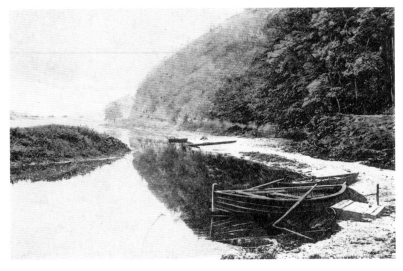

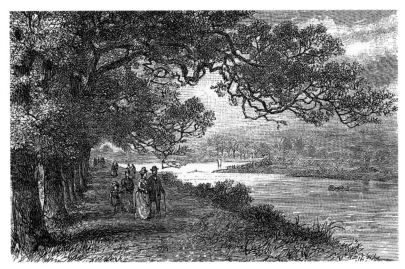

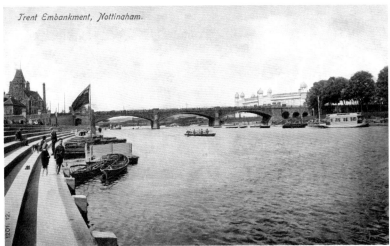

Above left: The ferry, Ratcliffe-on-Trent, early 1900s; a low-cost way across the river.

Above right: The Trent at Wilford, Nottingham in 1888.

Below left: The Trent Embankment looking towards Trent Bridge, early 1900s.

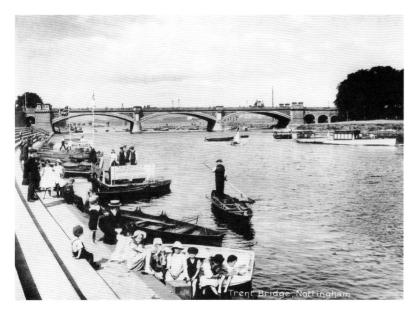

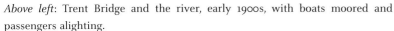

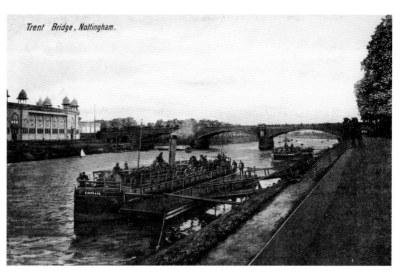

Above left: Trent Bridge and the river, early 1900s, with boats moored and passengers alighting.

Above right: Trent Bridge and recreational steamboats in the early 1900s.

Below right: Wilford Bridge around 1910 with its beautiful twin arches.

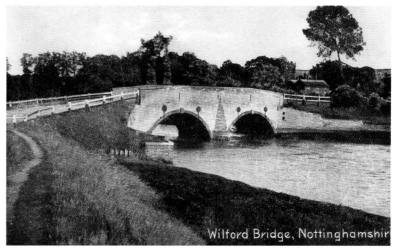

King's House at Clipston in Sherwood Forest which is today being rediscovered as a huge royal complex.

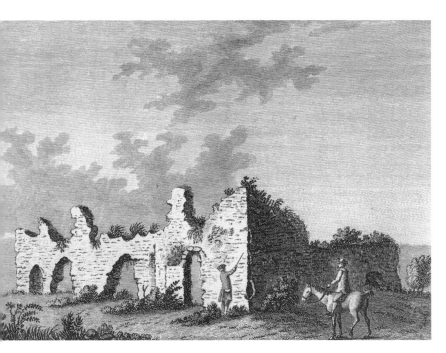

In Sherwood Forest – Victorian print.

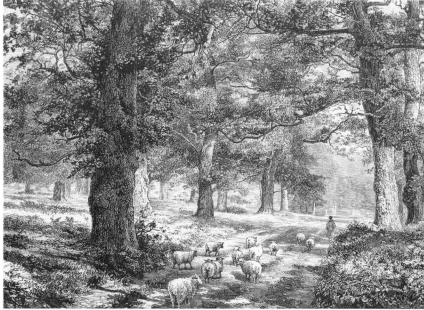

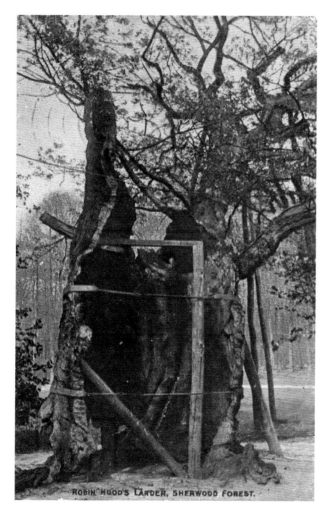

Robin Hood's Larder, Sherwood Forest, 1916.

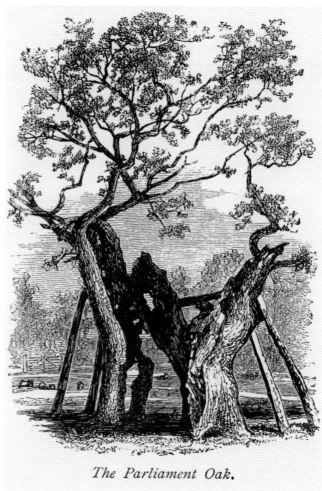

The Parliament Oak in the 1800s. It still remains today although only a shell of its former glory.

5

PEOPLE & PLACES: NOTTINGHAM FOLK & NOTTINGHAM NATTER

'I don't think I've left Nottingham altogether – I certainly never left it in my spirit.'

Alan Sillitoe, interviewed in 2008.

Central to activities in Nottingham was the Saturday Market, continuing an ancient privilege dating back to the reign of Henry II. The King granted a Royal Charter to the town declaring that the 'men of Nottinghamshire and Derbyshire were to come to the Borough of Nottingham every Friday and Saturday with their teams and pack horses'. By the reign of Henry VIII, antiquarian John Leland described the marketplace as 'the most fairest without exception in all England'. A somewhat later writer and commentator, John Evelyn, writing in 1654, noted that the marketplace was ample in size and had '... an open sough, a pond in its centre and a mouldering wall down its midst, with trees, saw-pits, stocks, pillory and ducking stool'. On the Long Row side and the west of the market were hardware, clothing, and the like, with down the east side, groceries, vegetables, corn, malt, oatmeal and salt. The south and to the west from the bottom of Mount Street and down Beastmarket Hill to South Parade

were swine, sheep, cattle and horses. In the centre were timber and joinery or carpentry materials, and to the east was the Women's Market with poultry and country produce. The southern side of the wall was a grassy bank with seven great elm trees until they were cut down in 1791. The town saw pits were located here on Timber Hill, and were important in the provision of sawn timber and planks for construction.

Nottingham people are friendly and welcoming, with a north-Midlands warmth, and Nottingham girls are supposed to be the prettiest in the country, or at least that is what they say! Furthermore, visitors, especially from overseas, may still be taken aback by a burly bus-driver addressing them as 'duck' or even 'duck-egg': 'Eh up mi duck' still being a standard greeting. The town still has a distance dialect and phrases or words descended in part from the ancient form of English spoken in the East Midlands.

However, in times past it was felt necessary to keep the ducking or cucking stool in the marketplace by the pond as a seventeenth-century punishment or deterrent for scolding refractory women, and dishonest tradesmen. The last recorded use was in 1619 when Widow Poynton was ducked in an attempt to stop her being a 'scold'. In all, Nottingham had five sets of stocks with one at the Shambles with a pillory adjacent to it. The last person publicly pilloried here was a Scotsman called Robert Calvin in 1808. Many of the offences which led to pillorying or the stocks were related to market trading: forestalling (i.e. buying up particular goods prior to the market opening in order to have a monopoly over sales), regrating (purchasing of goods at one price and then offering them for sale at an inflated price), the use of false weights, or the selling of inferior quality goods.

The sough, or drain, carried sewage and other material down from the properties at Long Row but was infilled with soil from nearby Gallows Hill some time roundabout 1826. The latter site is now the location of St Andrew's church on Mansfield Road.

The marketplace had three crosses, the Hen Cross close to the Poultry getting its name either from that or because it was the meeting place of women traders. By 1801 it had become dilapidated and reduced to just a pillar with a ball on top; so it was dismantled and the stones used for repairs to Trent Bridge. The Butter Cross, also known as Cheese Cross, was in front of the exchange, but was dismantled between 1714 and 1720. Finally, the Malt Cross was the most important and stood between Sheep Lane and St James Street. This was a large structure based on a series of steps and at its foot the maltsters and potters sold their wares, and they remained in this location until the early 1900s. However, the cross itself was demolished along with the remains of the market wall, sometime around 1714. This was followed by the resurfacing of the market to provide a good paved surface, and disputed between the town's authorities and local farmers as to who should pay for this luxury. One gesture from the authorities was to pay for the building of a new Malt Cross which had six pillars and came complete with a roof.

However, the arguments over tolls and fees to pay for the market went on for many years.

Yet the Cross remained a significant meeting point for a very long time. John and Charles Wesley preached here, banns of marriage were read here, and it was used as a place for official pronouncements. Miscreants were publicly whipped before the steps, and one man sold his seventeen-year-old wife and two children to another for 27s and 6d. Indeed, important announcements were made at the cross, such as when the Duke of Devonshire, Lord Delamere, Lord Howe, and the Earl of Stamford, along with other gentlemen, on 23 November 1688, publicly stated their acceptance of the Prince William of Orange, and his wife Queen Mary, as sovereigns in place of the Catholic-leaning James II. Eventually, on 11 October 1804, the second Malt Cross was removed, having become '... a public nuisance, a harbour for filth and rubbish, a resort for the idle, and a gaming place for apprentices...'.

Various changes continued throughout the history of the market, like for example, the introduction in January 1864, of gas lights to illuminate the stalls. The gas company were paid 6d per light in winter and 3d per light in summer. By this time markets were held every week on a Wednesday and a Saturday. Gradually what had been a chaotic scene became more organised and controlled, and for the Victorian market, after closing, each stallholder was responsible for taking down his or her stall and stacking the structures in a preordained space. This had to be to the satisfaction of the market bailiff, and only then could the whole place be swilled down and brushed clean.

Things move on and the coming of the electric tram was perhaps the beginning of the end for the old Market. Unlike horse-drawn transport the new tramways hemmed the market stalls into a confined space. The overall layout was altered and the wholesale fish-market was relocated at Sneinton. Despite the change, the stallholders continued and things returned to a sort of normality by the early 1900s with some even harbouring a fondness for the 'toast-racks' as the trams were affectionately known. However, the advent of the motorcar, the demolition of the old exchange in 1926, and the building of the new council house in the same year, consigned the old 5-acre market to history. Legend has it that when the old exchange was knocked down, one night a whole army of rats swarmed from the Shambles and up Friar Lane or Clumber Street, the only witness being a solitary policeman.

The Shambles was a dimly lit set of corridors under the old Exchange used by butchers. Each of the six corridors had its own name: Exchange Hall Shambles, Langley, Country, Jalland, North, and Hancock Shambles. Their combined rent in 1850 was £1,000 per year.

Modern Nottingham has grown out of a late twentieth-century post-industrial recession to become a regional centre for work and play, for health care, and for festivals, events, sports and pastimes.

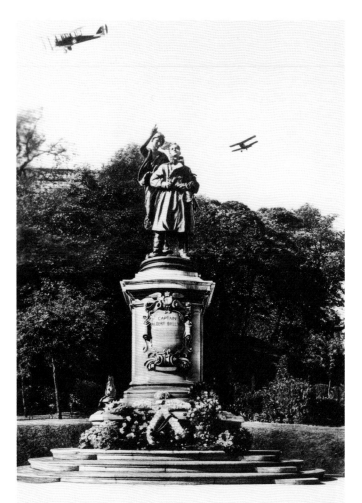

Captain Albert Ball V.C. Memorial. Castle Grounds

Captain Albert Ball VC Memorial in the Castle Grounds, early 1920s. He was an English fighter pilot during the First World War, and when he died was the UK's leading flying ace with forty-four victories to his name.

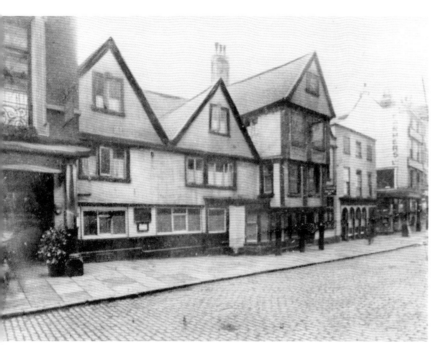

Goose Fair, Nottingham on the original site before 1909.

1920s' view of the Flying Horse Hotel, described as situated upon The Poultry and located where the Pumptre family built a house in the 1200s.

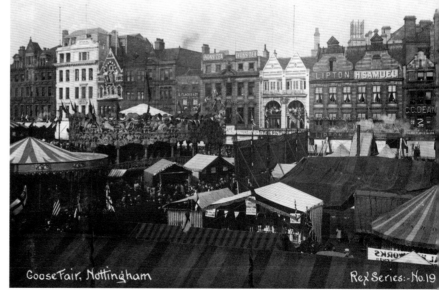

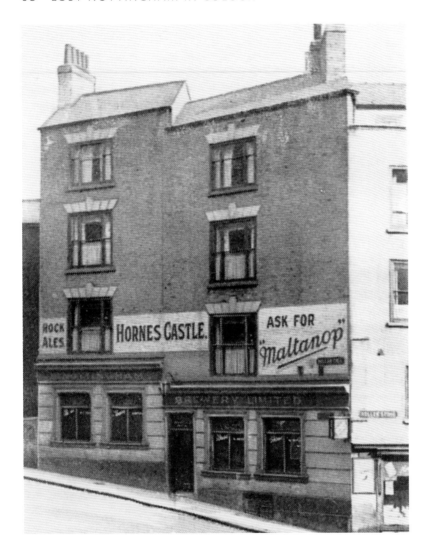

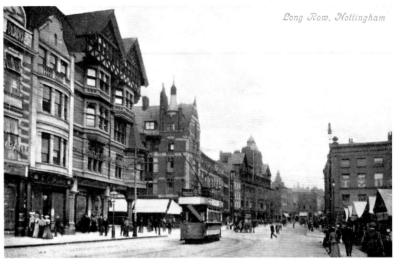

Above: Long Row, Nottingham, in the early Edwardian period, a wide commercial thoroughfare with electric trams.

Left: Horne's Castle in Hollow Stone in the 1920s, formerly the residence of William Andrew Horne Esquire, in 1729, who, on the morning of his seventy-fourth birthday, was hanged for murder.

Opposite: Market Place, Nottingham, 1800s.

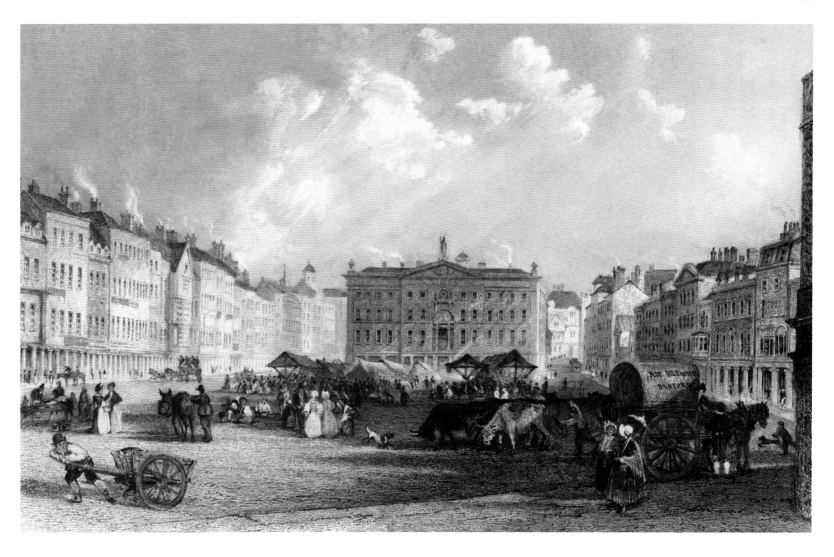

Market Place, with the largest open market area in England at 5½ acres, early 1900s.

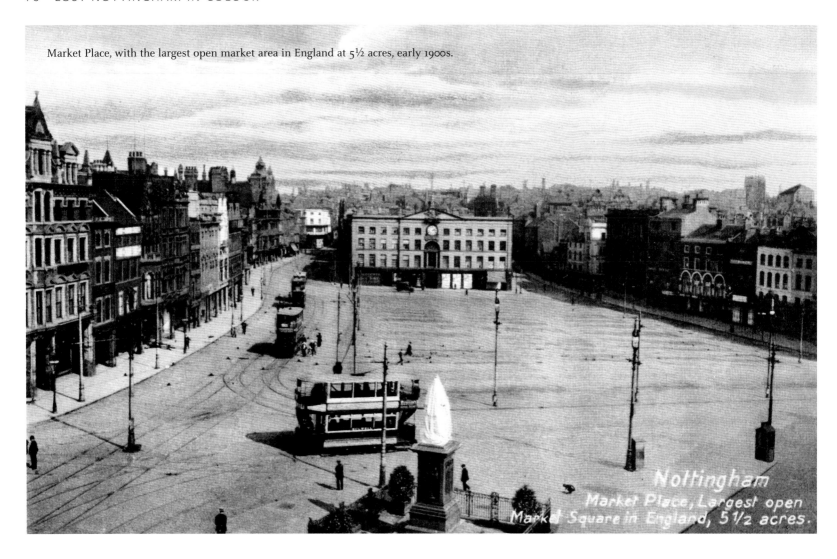

Nottingham
Market Place, Largest open
Market Square in England, 5½ acres.

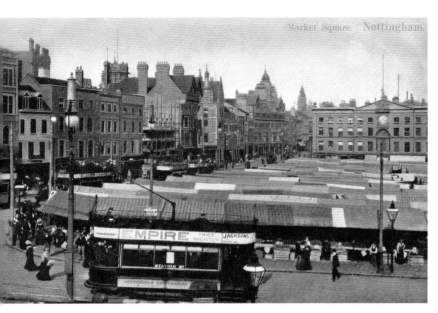

A busy Market Square with stalls and trams, early 1900s.

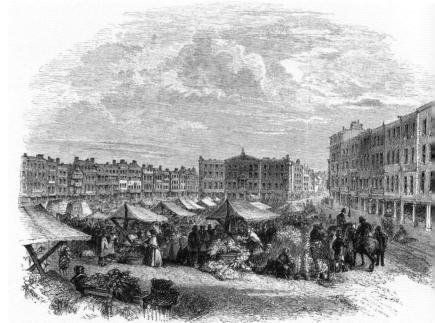

The hustle and bustle of a rather disorganised market place and exchange, Nottingham, 1800s.

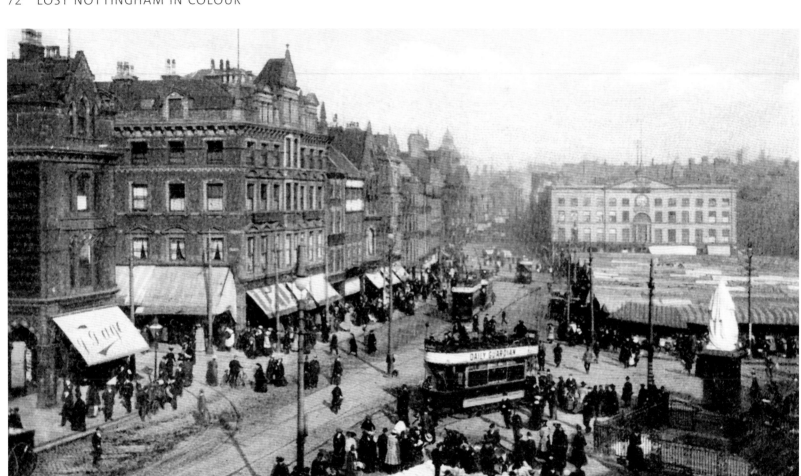

Nottingham market, around 1908.

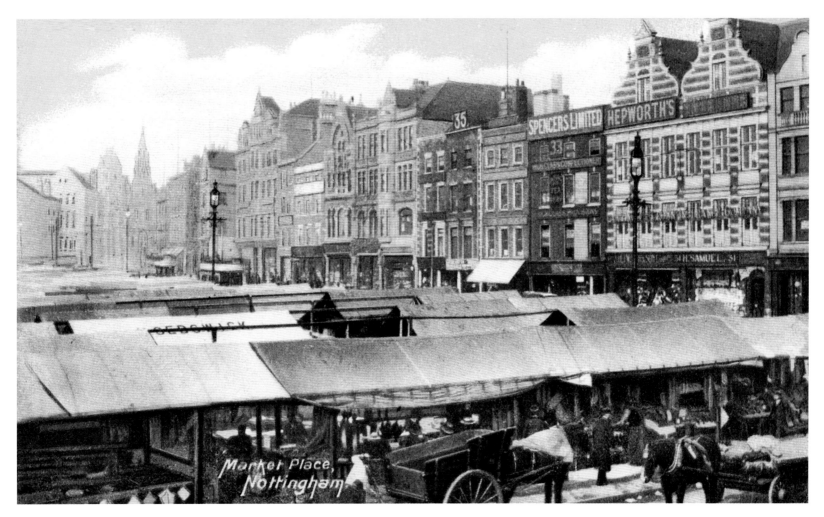

Nottingham market place with wagons, vendors and shoppers, early 1900s.

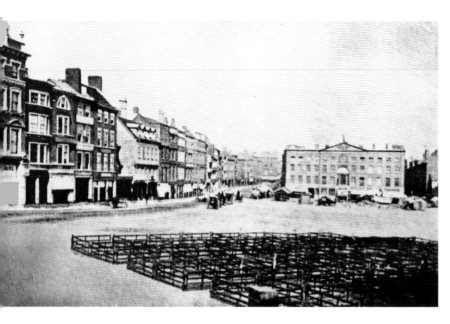

The beast market awaiting its beasts, around 1865.

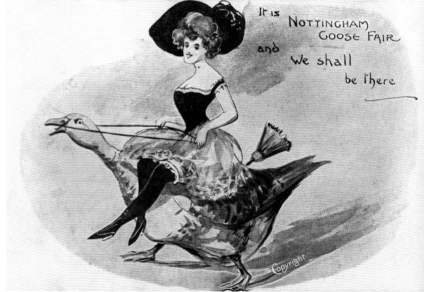

The goose fair and a Nottingham lass in 1909.

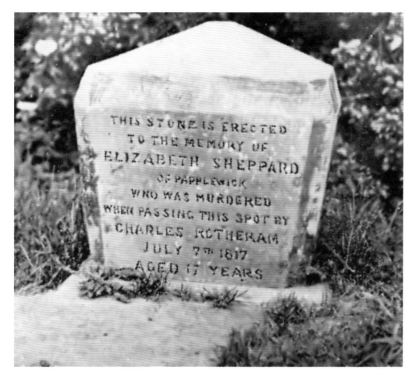

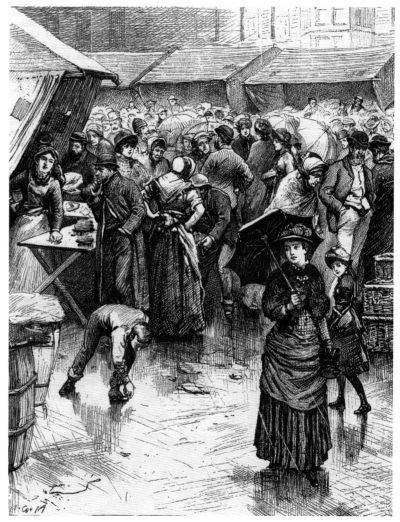

Above: The Murder Stone as a memorial on Mansfield Road to mark the spot where Elizabeth Sheppard, aged seventeen, was murdered by Charles Rotheram on 7 July 1817.

Right: The market place, Nottingham, 1884.

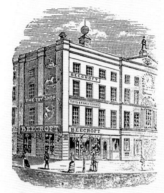

Presents! Presents!

NOTTINGHAM EXCHANGE.

When we were boys,
We bought our Toys
at
BEECROFT'S.

Now we are men,
We'll go again
to
BEECROFT'S.

For all the Latest Novelties in

TOYS,
GAMES AND FANCY GOODS

GO TO

Beecroft & Sons, Exchange Corner,

MARKET PLACE, NOTTINGHAM.

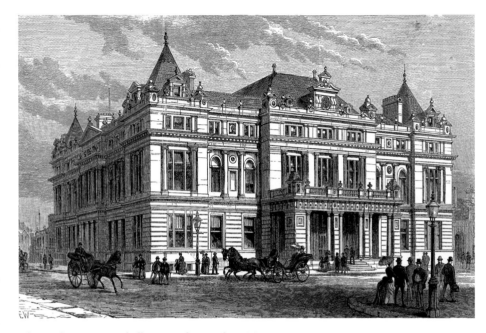

Above: The new town hall, Nottingham, July 1988.

Left: Victorian toyshop advert.

6

PARKS & GARDENS

Overlooked by its castle on the hill, Nottingham has a wealth of open spaces, from Victorian parks to botanical gardens, and from libraries, museums to art galleries and theatres. Wollaton Hall, built in 1588 by Sir Francis Willoughby (1547–1596), and its wonderful parkland of red deer, is a dramatic connection and reminder of an historic past. The hall houses significant collections of paintings and a natural history museum, and the grounds include the Camelia House, the oldest cast-iron building in Britain. Over the years, Wollaton Park has been host to many events and celebrations with Salvation Army parades and other religious activities, archery competitions, and dog handling shows. One particularly unusual period was when the park was home to German prisoners of war distinguished by their uniforms with 'P' in large print on the back. Also in the 1940s, the park was a temporary home to the US 508th Parachute Regiment. This is just one of the special open spaces within the city. Furthermore, Nottingham seems to embrace the idea of tree-lined avenues and wide open roads. With museums, galleries and parks aplenty, the city is well placed to provide a good quality of life for its residents.

Around Nottingham Castle was Nottingham Park or 'Coney Garth' i.e. a rabbit warren to supply the castle with meat and fur. As a park, the area had deer and also fishponds, again to provide food but also sport to the castle's occupants. Deer were last kept here in 1717, but they were hunted as 'carted' deer until the 1790s. Gradually, with the demise of the original functions of the park, the area began to be converted to fashionable housing but still with substantial greenspace. The statue of Robin Hood by James Woodford was erected by the castle in 1952.

As industry grew in the 1800s, the expanding, dirty city, like many in Victorian England, sprawled out across the countryside subsuming all before it. However, the industrial barons realised the benefits of open spaces and exercise, and provided extensive parks and gardens, and many remain to this day. Furthermore, many of Nottingham's major routes through the city have lines of splendid avenue street-trees.

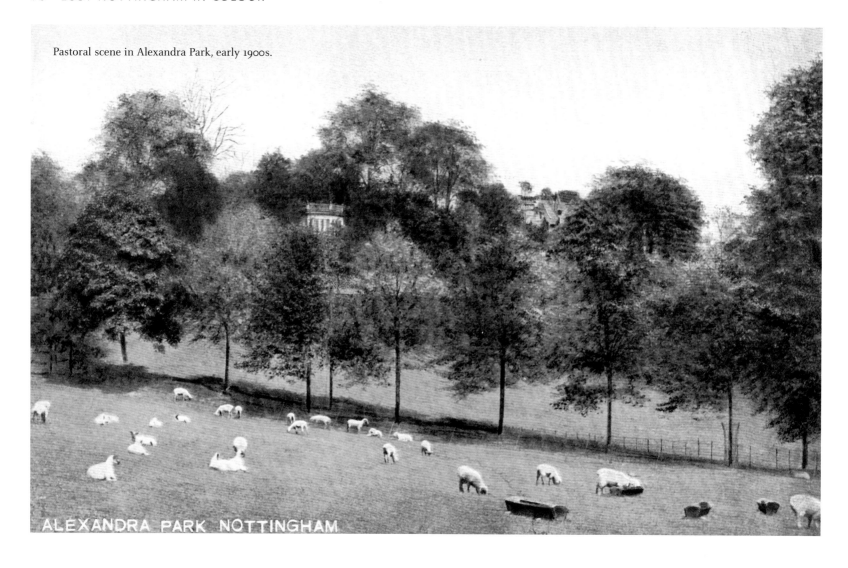

Pastoral scene in Alexandra Park, early 1900s.

Boulevard and Landing Stage, Nottingham in around 1900.

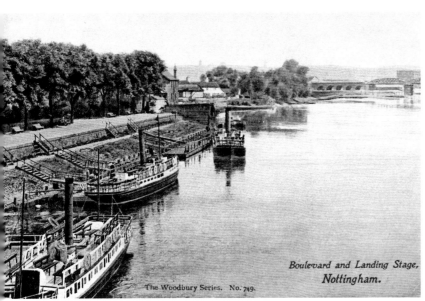

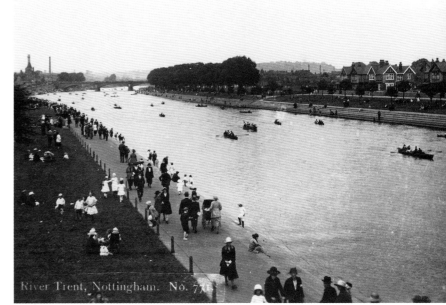

Boating on the River Trent at Nottingham in the 1920s.

Wollaton Hall, 1906.

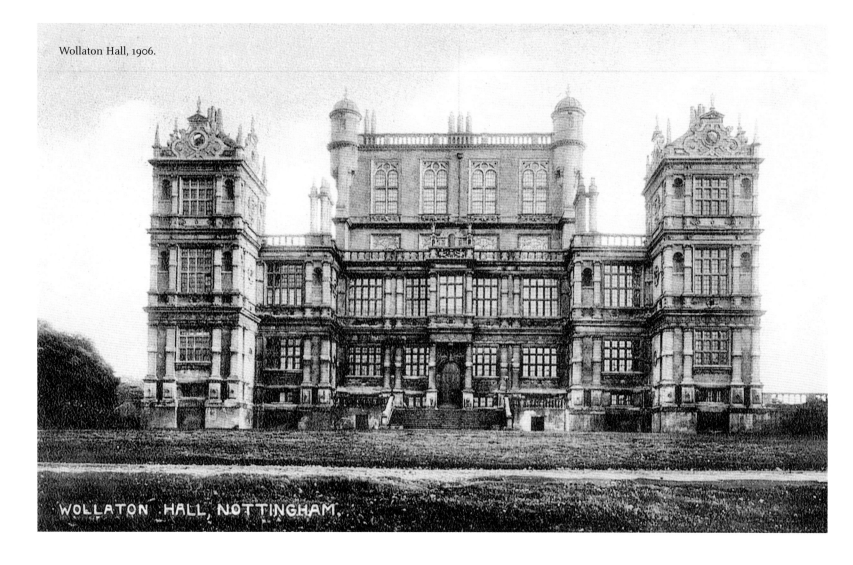

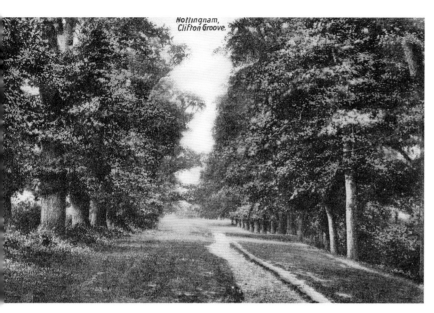

A view of a verdant avenue at Clifton Grove in the early 1900s.

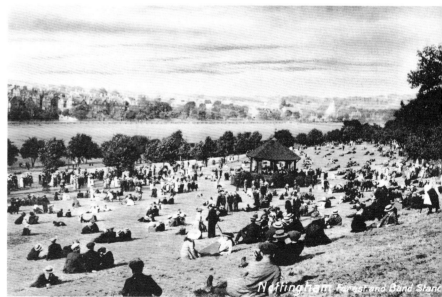

The parks and open spaces in Victorian towns were hugely popular recreational places. This postcard, sent 3 October 1914, depicts the Forest and band stand.

Lenton Boulevard as the town expanded across the land in front of the old castle, 1888.

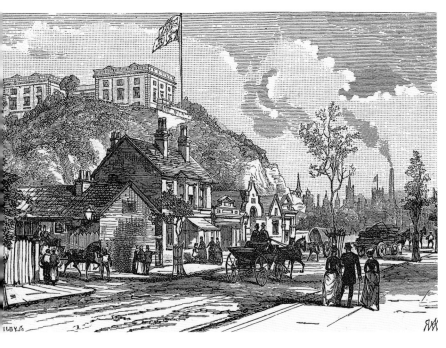

Nottingham Castle and grounds in the 1970s, by this time, a sizeable area of urban parkland.

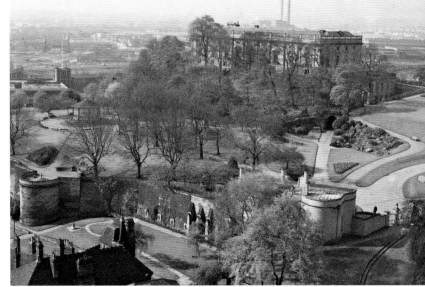

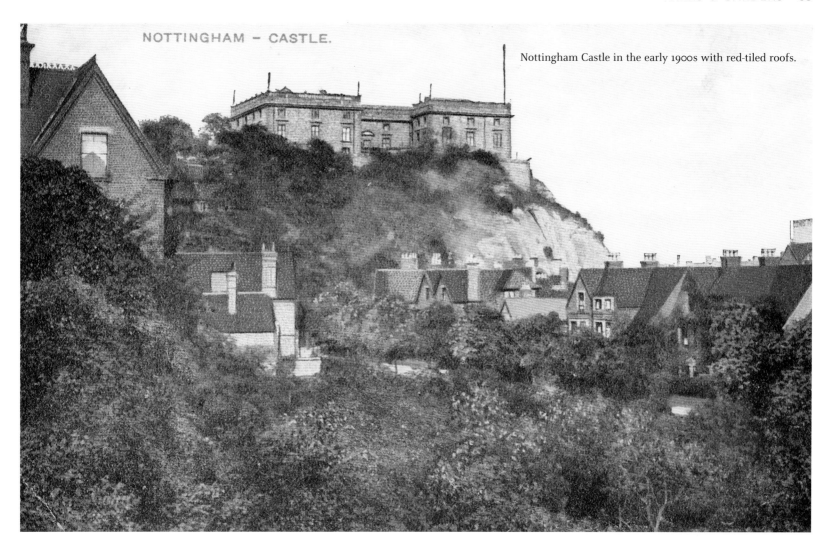

NOTTINGHAM – CASTLE.

Nottingham Castle in the early 1900s with red-tiled roofs.

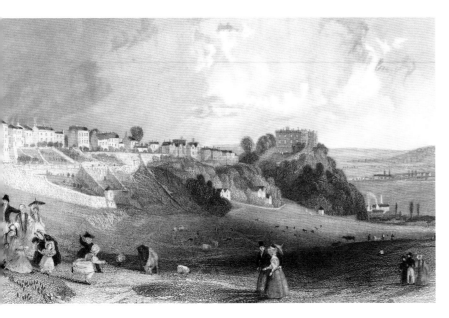

Local folk enjoying a day out at Nottingham Park, 1800s.

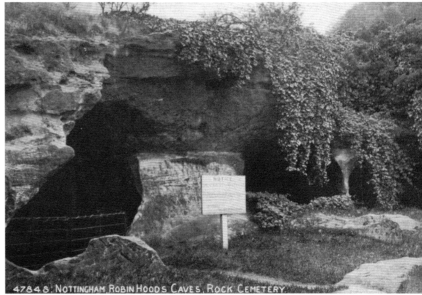

Robin Hood's Caves and Rock Cemetery, Nottingham, early 1900s.

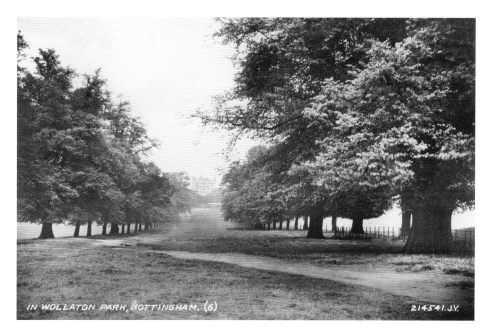

IN WOLLATON PARK, NOTTINGHAM. (6)   214541.J.Y.

Above: The famous Avenue, Wollaton Park, 1931.

Right: The Arboretum, Nottingham, one of the many green spaces in the growing city, *c.* 1920s.

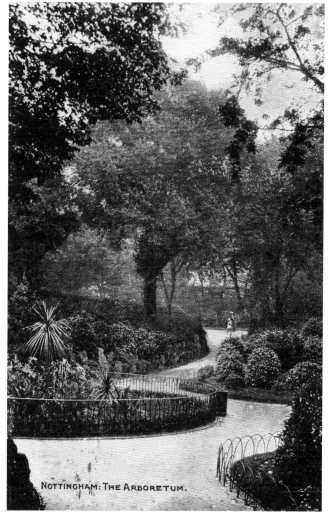

NOTTINGHAM: THE ARBORETUM.

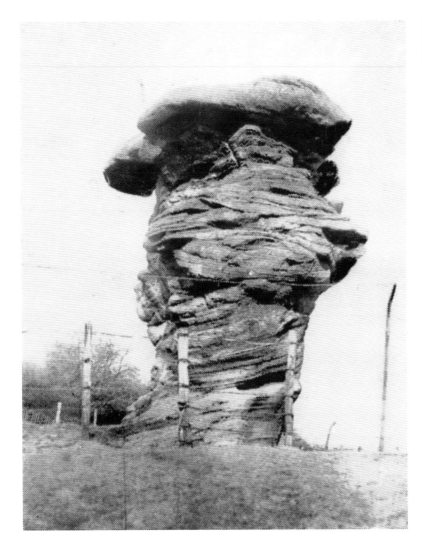

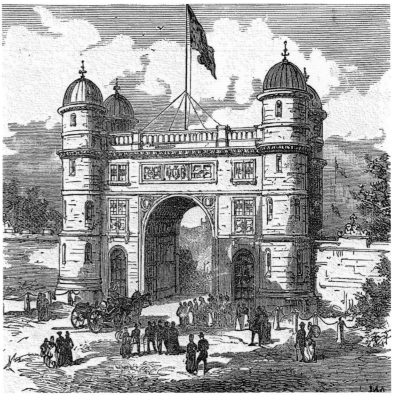

Above: The Entrance Gateway at Wollaton Park, Nottingham, 1888.

Left: The famous Hemlock Stone, photographed in the 1920s.

Opposite: The Hemlock Stone, taken around 1905.

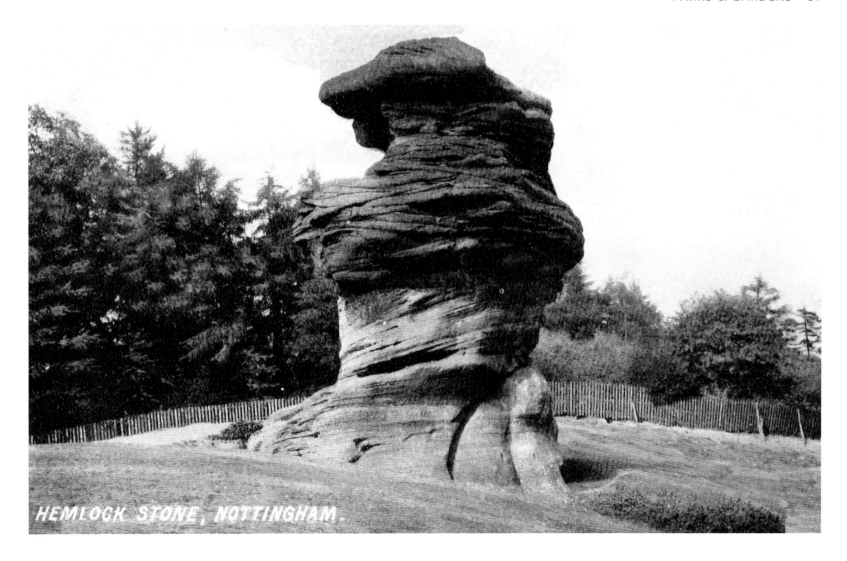

HEMLOCK STONE, NOTTINGHAM.

The Park, Nottingham, in 1888, with the spread of grand Victorian houses and tennis courts in the foreground.

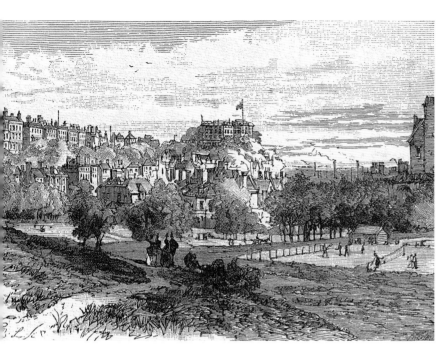

The Promenade from Trent Bridge, Nottingham, 1888.

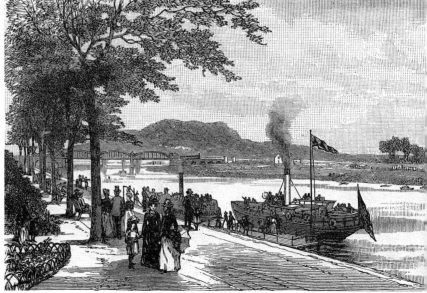

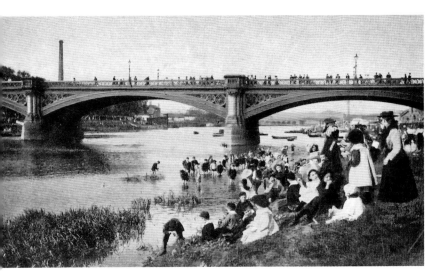

Trent Bridge with crowd and bathers, early 1900s.

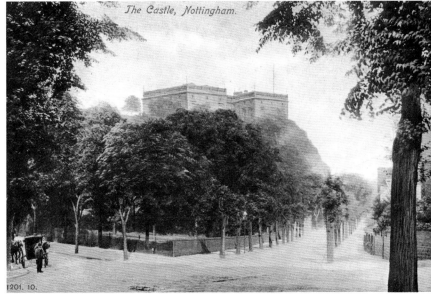

The Castle, Nottingham.

1201. 10.

View of the castle in around 1900.

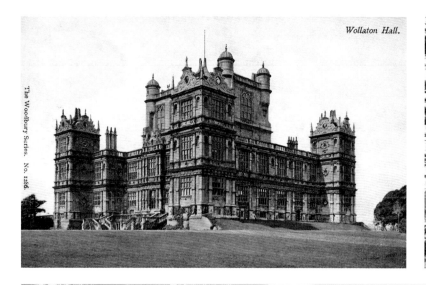

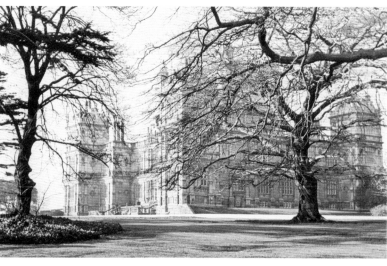

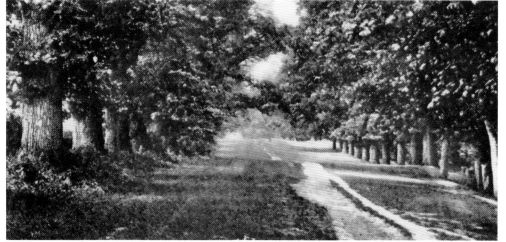

Above left: Wollaton Hall in the early 1900s.

Above right: Wollaton Park in the 1970s, by Mrs D. Smith.

Below left: Clifton Grove, planted around 1740, provides a sylvan romantic walk and used to have itinerant fiddlers and singers.

7

EDUCATION & HEALTH

With its importance as a medieval administrative centre, Nottingham always had good provision for basic needs. However, as the industrial city grew, the demand for education and improvement of its population became obvious. The need for specialist skills, training and research for the new industries leading Nottingham's industrial revolution meant schools, colleges, universities, libraries, and art galleries all flourished. Then, with rising population, there was the demand for improved health care and hospitals. Early provision of hospitals or almshouses for example, were often based on bequests and support from wealthy and enlightened philanthropists like Anne Burton. The workhouse for example, which had replaced the old city workhouse when the Victoria Station was built, became Bagthorpe Hospital and then Nottingham City Hospital. A general hospital was constructed in 1782. Today, Nottingham has one of the leading teaching hospitals in the country, the Queen's Medical Centre, opened in 1970, being one of the largest hospitals in the UK, and indeed one of the biggest teaching hospitals in Europe.

From modest beginnings in the nineteenth century, higher education in Nottingham is delivered through two top-class universities in Nottingham University and Nottingham Trent. The University College became Nottingham University in 1948. Indeed today, the combined universities contribute a major part of Nottingham's population and a great deal of its wealth.

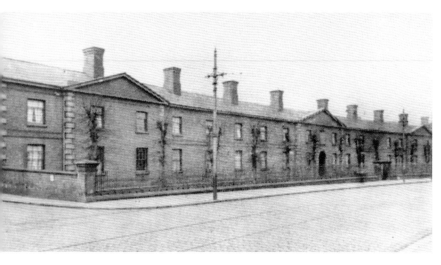

Burton's Almshouses on London Road in the 1920s, established with a bequest from Miss Ann Burton of Spaniel Row in the 1850s.

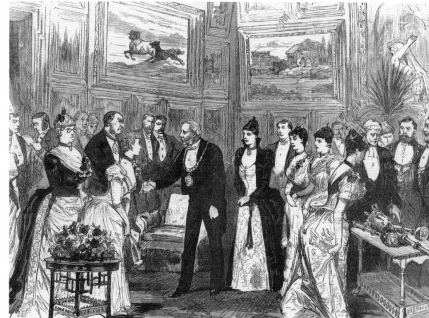

Conversazione at the museum, Nottingham Castle, 6 October 1877.

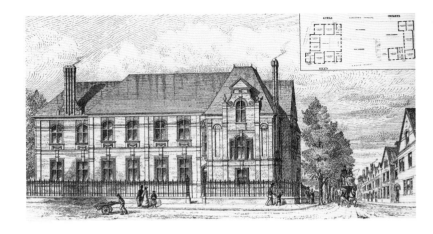

Architect's drawing of Nottingham School Board, Hungar Hill Road School, 1879.

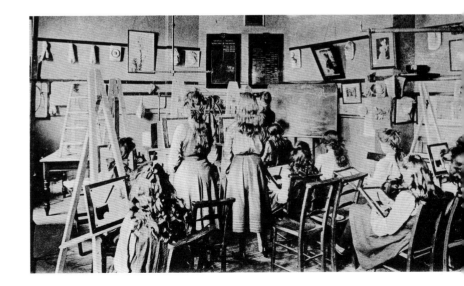

Nottingham High School for Girls, *c.* 1900.

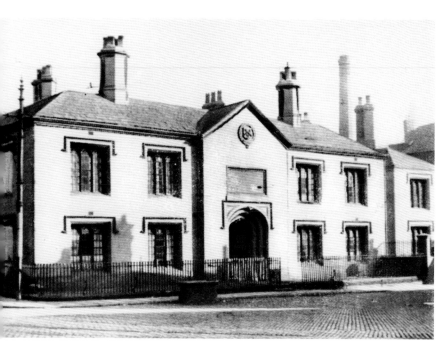

Plumptre Hospital, Plumptre Square, shown in the 1920s and originally founded in 1392 by John de Plumptre.

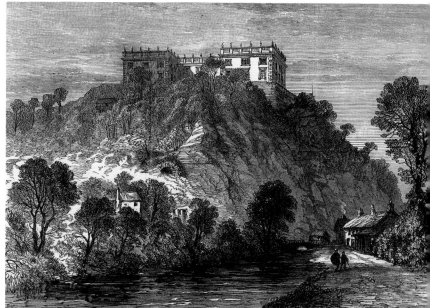

The Midland Counties Art Museum, Nottingham Castle, west front pictured in the 1800s.

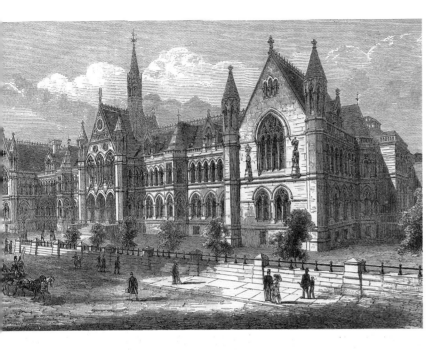

The planned new University College, Nottingham, in the process of being erected in 1877.

The new University College, 1888.

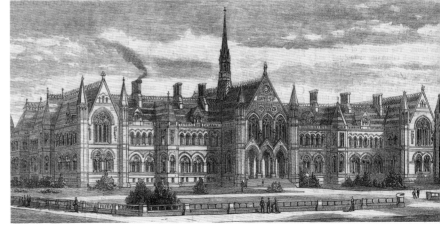

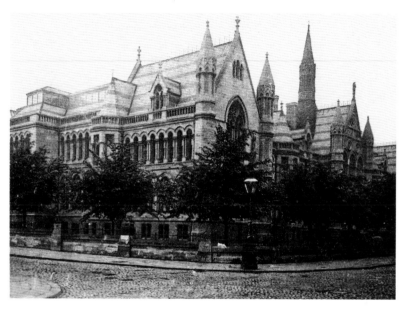

University College, Nottingham, c. 1903.

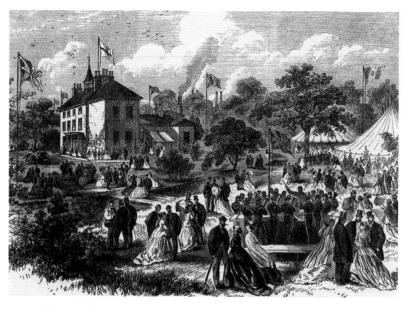

Visit of the British Association to Basford Park, Nottingham, 1866.

8

TRANSPORT & URBAN CONDITIONS

For more than a millennium visitors from the south would have crossed the River Trent at the main Trent Bridge. The earliest record crossing here was built for King Edward the Elder in about 920 AD. A medieval replacement to this early structure lasted until 1871 when it was replaced; though the medieval arches survive in part on a traffic island. The old Trent Bridge was known as Hethbeth Bridge, and with seventeen arches was 668 feet long. Built mostly of brick the structure rested on oak piles driven deep into the riverbed. The new bridge with three arches was sufficient until the 1920s when it was deemed to be too narrow, and was widened. Additional widening occurred in the late twentieth century. Trent Bridge was completely within the jurisdiction of Nottingham until 1952 when the boundary changed to become the centre of the river. Until local government changes in the 1870s, the boundary between West Bridgford and Nottingham went right through the Trent Bridge Inn. Apparently during the medieval beating of the bounds, the Mickleton jury climbed in through one window and left via another. The inn has another claim to fame in that in 1838 a certain William Clarke, who had married the landlady of the Trent Bridge Inn, went on to establish the now-famous county and Test cricket ground.

Nowadays, half the bridge is in the Meadows District, named after the medieval common meadows on the fertile flood-land of the Trent. This was about the time that the Anglo-Saxon settlement of Nottingham was established on the high sandstone cliff about one mile further north beyond the river. In times past the old road linking the bridge to the town was called the Flood Road, and, of course, the Meadows were frequently inundated too. Indeed, whilst in a dry summer you could sometimes walk across the river on stones on the river bottom, in winter the Trent might flood from West Bridgford to the Meadows. The major urbanisation began here in the 1860s with the new estate and roads like Arkwright Street. Bad flooding occurred in 1947 but since then works have been done to keep the water at bay, though for how long it is hard to say as climate change is tipping the balance.

As Nottingham grew and transportation developed, the road networks reached ever outwards from the old town to the peripheral villages, hamlets, and townships. Over the centuries, horse-drawn carriage, horse and cart, and walking, gave way to trams, buses, and then the motorcar. However, for transportation for industry and commerce, along with roads there were canals and rail, and of course the river. Today, Nottingham is well served by the nearby East Midlands airport. The developing roads extended across the flatlands to unite formerly separate communities, but until the toll-charging turnpikes, many roads were almost impassable with surfaces poor, muddy and rutted, and maintenance minimal. However, by the 1700s and 1800s, toll-charging turnpikes were de rigueur and new, often straight roads cut directly through the newly-enclosed countryside; a new order was imposed. Then, with innovation in road surfacing, which moved away from stones collected by the rural poor, to limestone chippings for macadam surfaces. Tarmacadam soon followed and the modern roadway was born. Modern Nottingham has the M1 motorway right on its western doorstep.

However, the spiritual centre of Nottingham's transport system has been, and in many ways still is, the great River Trent, the artery for a city and a community.

By 1796, Nottingham canal was connecting to Langley Mill and hence the Cromford Canal and industrial Derbyshire. Like many such ventures, the Canals have survived in part, though their heyday was short-lived because of the advent of rail.

The arrival of the railway in 1839 meant a big increase in traffic taking the southern routes in to the Market Place and this led to a review of the transport routes to the Midland Station. The decision was taken to widen and improved streets like Wheeler Gate, Lister Gate and Carrington Street. Some like Wheeler Gate were incredibly narrow, almost medieval streets, more alleyways than roads. Left until about 1885, Wheeler Gate became almost impassable to traffic and so drastic action was needed. First of all it was widened within the boundaries of adjacent properties, but by 1892, this was still not sufficient. Properties on the eastern side of the road were demolished and a reasonable, functioning width was achieved. Replacement new premises were established further back from the road. This was not always achieved without dispute since some proprietors, such as Lamb's hosiery shop, objected to the interference with their businesses.

The problems were almost insuperable, with transport becoming rapidly mired down. Lister Gate was described as a narrow, filthy barrier to traffic and little more than a swamp at its junction with Broad Marsh. However, in 1864, the properties on either side were demolished, the street widened, and the road surface was raised significantly. Some businesses were very concerned as the works progressed towards them, an example being Jalland's Hotel. The solution in their case was to remove the building brick by brick a distance of twelve feet to the rear and onto the new building line. It was even suggested that they might move the entire building intact, but sadly this spectacular feat was never attempted.

The route to the station continued from Greyfriar Gate down Carrington Street, a road laid out in 1829 and named after Lord Carrington. The latter was a descendant of the founder of Collins Hospital which stood at the northwest end of the road. Following alterations to Canal Street, Carrington became one of Nottingham's busiest thoroughfares; enough to merit its own policeman on traffic duty, and one of only twelve in the town. A bridge over the canal built in 1841, took traffic up and to the station. This cost £6,000 and was constructed by Corts Iron-Founders of Park Street, Nottingham, with the expense split between the Midland Railway Company and the town.

Nottingham centre itself has been transformed with major works occurring during the Victorian expansion and then again in the mid- to late twentieth century. Opened by the mayor at the Goose Fair in 1865, but named Theatre Street, Market Street as it was soon called, transformed access out of the market to the town beyond. The route out of the site had previously been Sheep Lane, a narrow and winding street which made movement of vehicles particularly problematic. Nottingham centre had gas lights in 1819, but it remained dirty and unsanitary, and had a cholera epidemic in 1833 killing 330 people. With the appointment in 1873 of the town's first medical officer, rationalisation of transport and access issues went hand-in-hand with slum clearance and improvements to sanitation. Modern-day Nottingham was gradually emerging from the randomness of the medieval and the squalor of the urban Victorian.

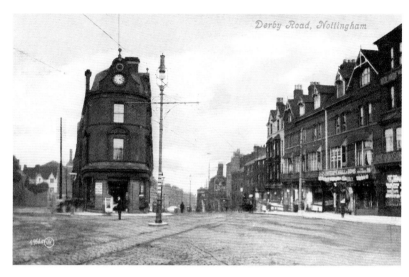

Above: Derby Road, Nottingham, 1906.

Right: Gordon House, Wildman Street, Nottingham, in the early 1900s.

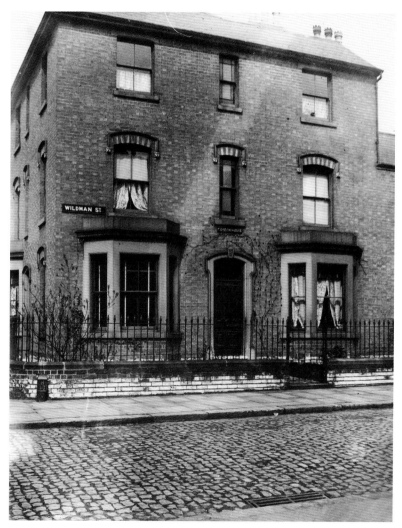

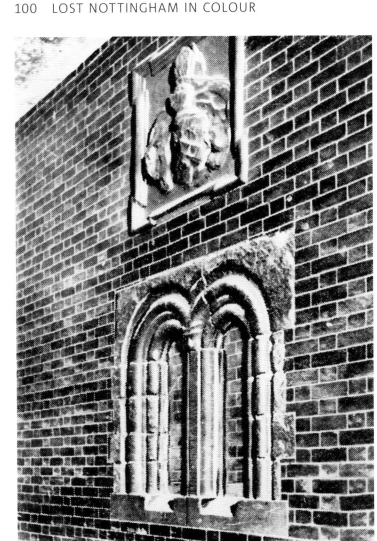

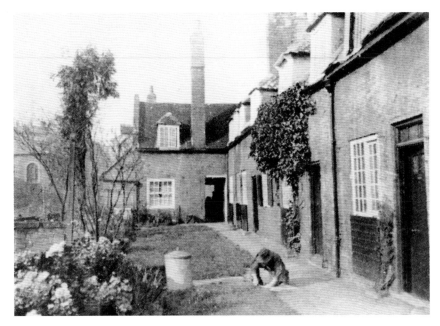

Above: Jasmine Cottages – formerly Workhouse Yard, on Castle Road, pictured in the 1920s.

Left: Norman arches preserved in the modern wall at Broadway, pictured in the 1920s.

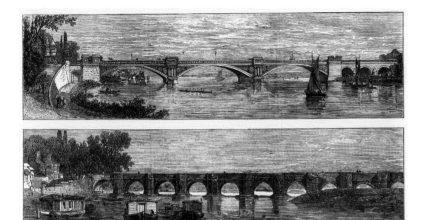

Above: Nottingham Bridge old and new pictured in 1869.

Right: North side of Parliament Street in the 1890s.

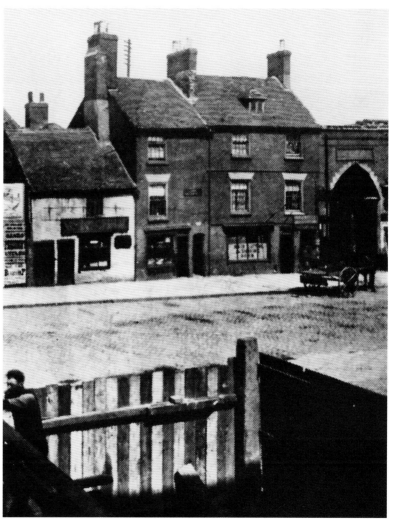

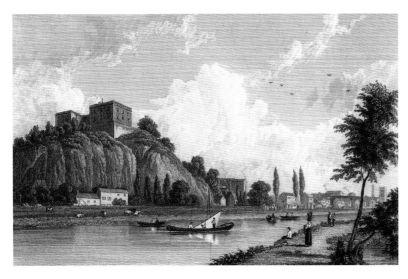

Nottingham in the late 1700s with rowing boats, sailing boats and a woman carrying a basket on her head.

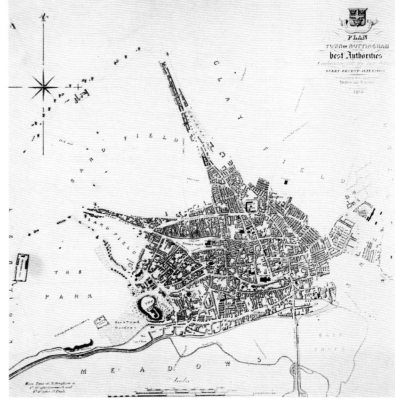

Nottingham, mapped by Dearden in 1835.

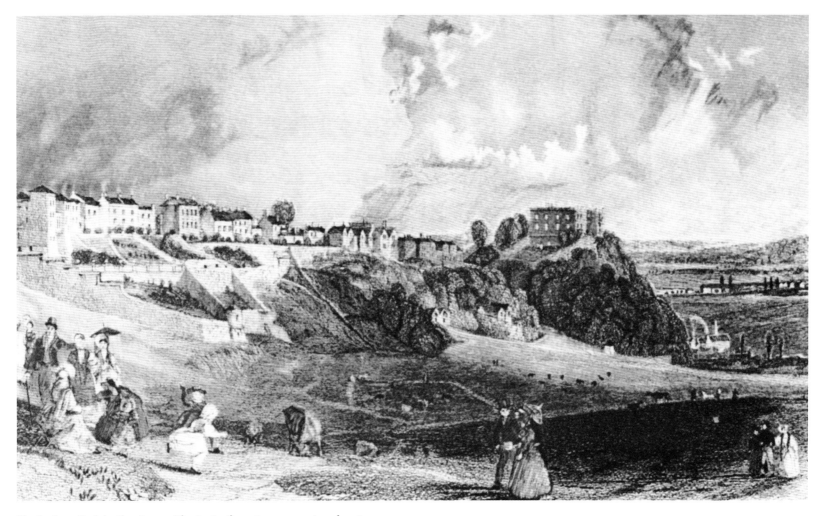

Nottingham Park in the 1800s with nineteeth-century expansion showing.

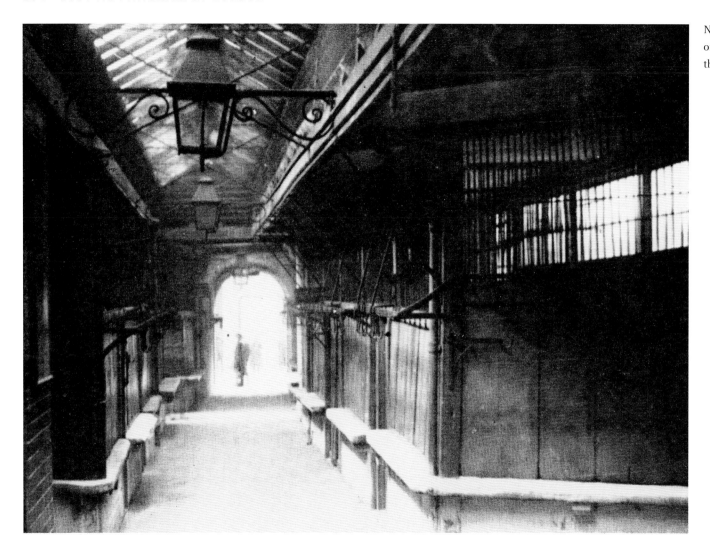

Nottingham Shambles, or butchers' shops, in the late 1800s.

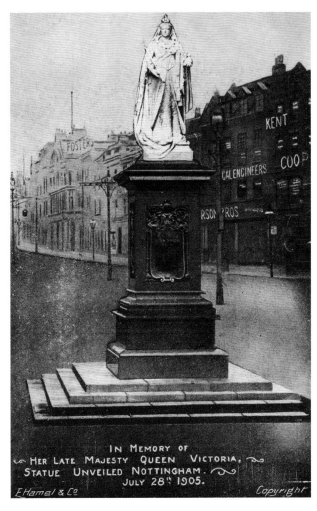

Queen Victoria Memorial, 1905.

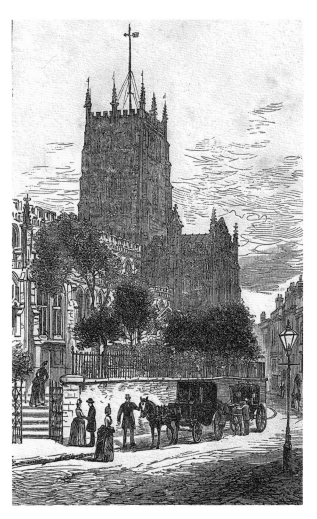

St Mary's church, 1888.

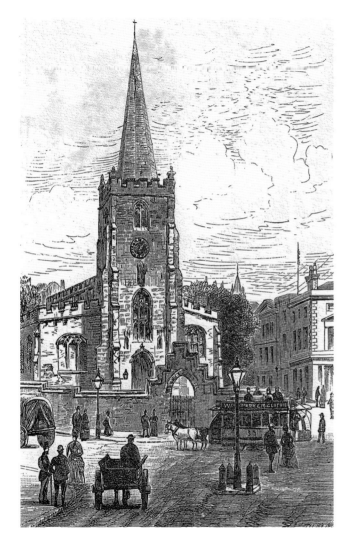

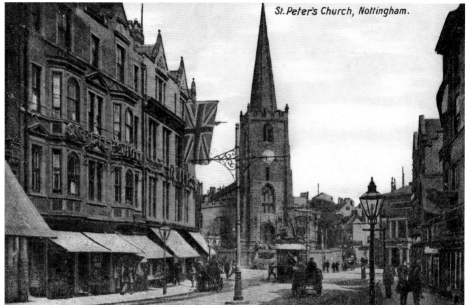

Above: St Peter's church, early 1900s.

Left: St Peter's church, 1888.

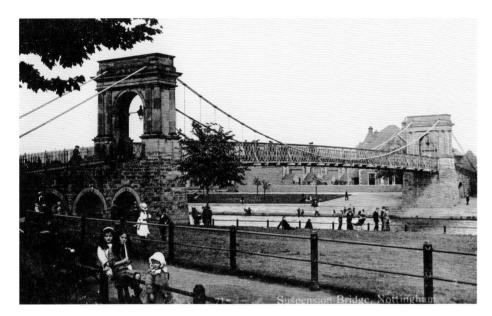

Above: Suspension Bridge, Nottingham, *c.* 1920s.

Right: A sweet-shop advert from 1901. With sugar becoming increasingly available, sweets were becoming popular.

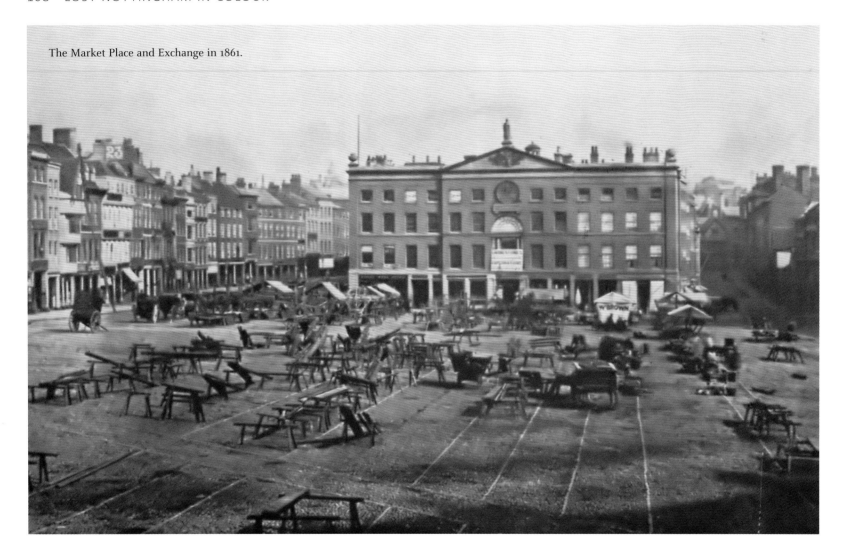

The Market Place and Exchange in 1861.

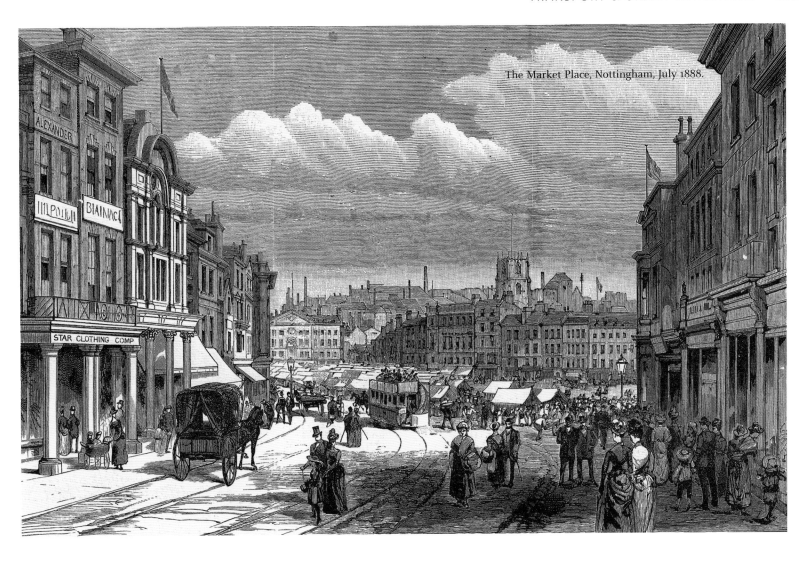

The Market Place, Nottingham, July 1888.

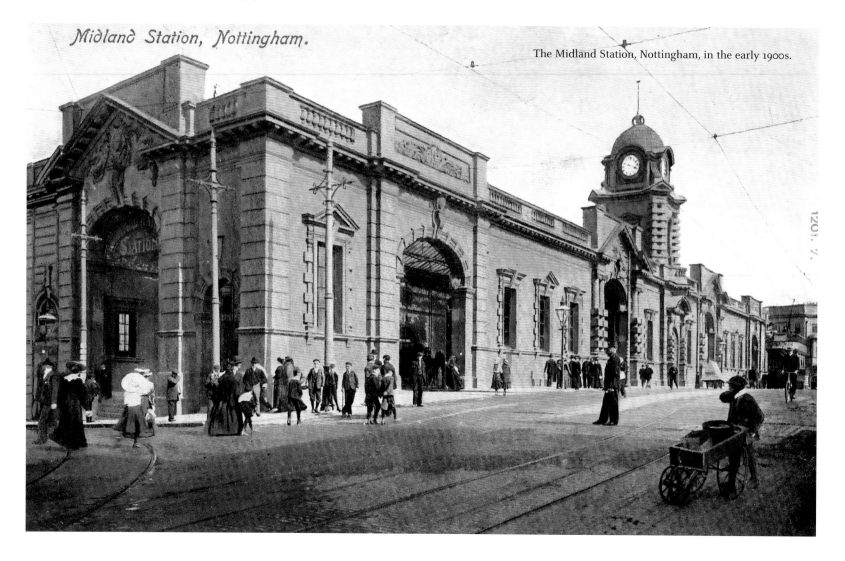

The Midland Station, Nottingham, in the early 1900s.

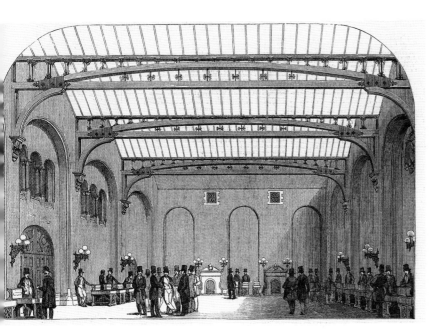

The New Corn Exchange, Nottingham, 1850.

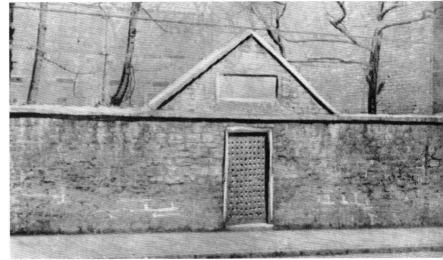

The separate Jews' Graveyard, Sherwood Street photographed in the 1920s and established in 1823 at the request of the Jewish community.

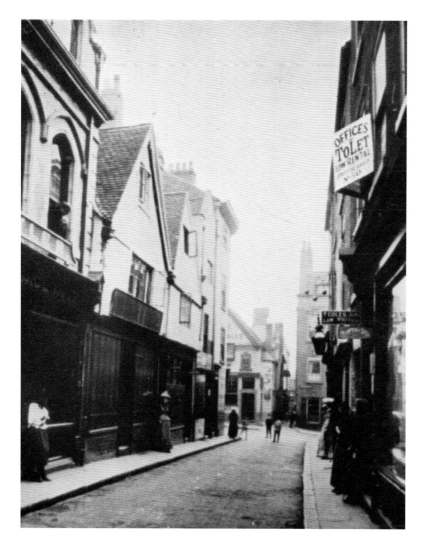

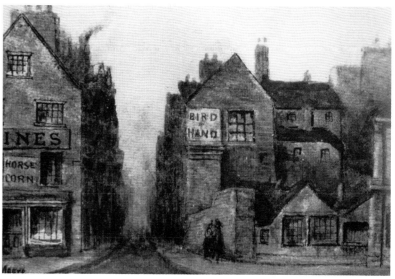

Above: The top of Sheep Lane from Parliament Street in 1860.

Left: The southern end of Bridlesmith Gate in 1900.

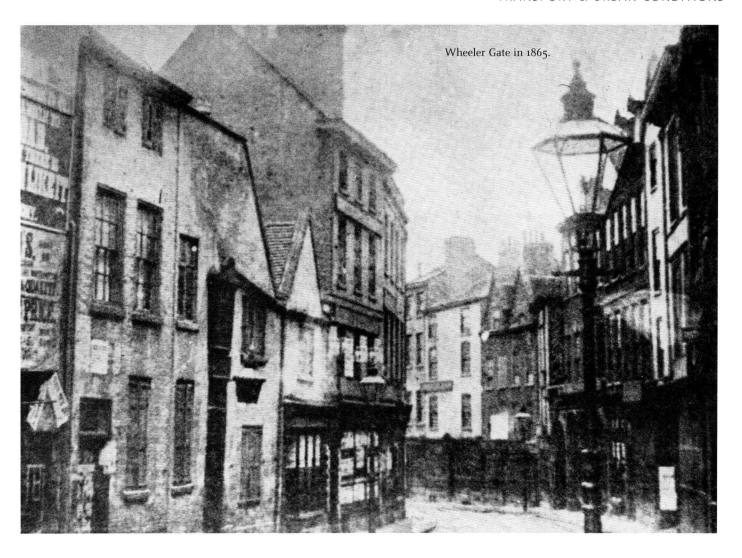

Wheeler Gate in 1865.

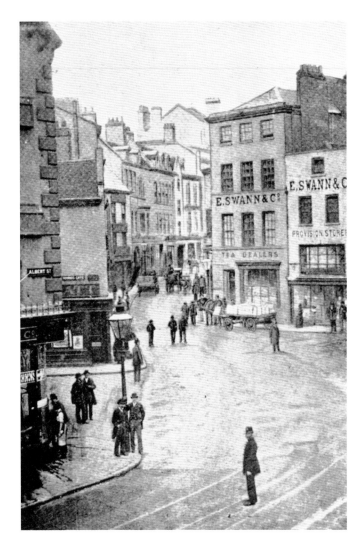

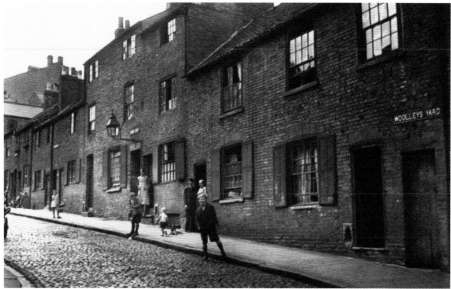

Above: Woolleys Yard, Nottingham, about 1933.

Left: Wheeler Gate in 1886, after the first phase of road widening.

9

SPORTS, THEATRE, ARTS & CULTURE

Nottingham boasts two major professional football clubs in Forest and County, the former in relatively recent times dominating the English League and even European competitions. With a county cricket ground at Trent Bridge, the city hosts both county and Test matches throughout the summer. There are venues for rugby union, ice hockey, basketball, and water sports too. The National Water Sports Centre was constructed to open in 1973.

The city has rich traditions in music, theatre and other popular entertainments. At night, with local people and the student populations of two big universities, the city centre comes alive with a heady mix of club goers and theatre or music lovers. From the 1760s with streets now lit by oil lamps, Nottingham's first theatre was built. Around two centuries later, the Nottingham Playhouse Theatre opened in 1963, having been first established as a repertory theatre in 1948 in the former Goldsmith Street cinema. Nottingham today is truly a city of the twenty-first century with vibrant theatres, especially the Theatre Royal, staging music and shows to suit all tastes. Old theatres have includes venues such as the Royal Hippodrome which opened in 1908.

The most famous pub here is perhaps the Old Trip To Jerusalem Inn at Brewhouse Yard and described as an 'ancient pub built into stone caves with a charming, wonky interior and resident ghosts, plus food'. Dating from 1189 AD it claims to be the oldest pub in England. Nottingham has long been home to great beers and wonderful pubs, a number dating back many centuries. Some, such as The Gate Hangs Well on Castle Road at the corner of Brewhouse Yard, were demolished, this one in 1909. An ancient rhyme celebrated the old pub: 'This gate hangs well and hinders none, refresh and pay, and travel on'. Demolished about the same time was the Postern Gate on what is now the main route into the Broad Marsh Centre.

With its reputation for good beers and pubs, is it any wonder that William Booth, the son of Samuel Booth, born in Nottingham on 10 April 1829, in Sneinton, went on to become the founder of the Salvation Army. One convert was Tom o' the Fens, a convicted poacher.

Nottingham grew rapidly during the 1900s, with the 1920s and 1930s witnessing massive Council Estates built by Nottingham City Council north of the old city. More followed in the 1950s and 1960s including Bilborough, and in the south, Clifton. It was the time of urban expansion and industrialisation of the countryside which so affected D. H. Lawrence, born in Eastwood in 1885, and growing up in the area. The son of a former school teacher and a Nottinghamshire coalminer, David Herbert Lawrence was brought up in the small mining community of Eastwood, and went on to be one of the most influential writers of the twentieth century, though at times somewhat rabidly right-wing. Whilst despising democracy, liberalism, socialism, egalitarianism, and the masses, at the same time he considered the dehumanising effects of modernity and industrialisation,

The human soul needs beauty more than bread.

D. H. Lawrence

This is a sentiment which is okay unless you are hungry! Controversial and contradictory to the end, Lawrence died young at only forty-four years of age. The combination of Sillitoe, Byron, and Lawrence places Nottingham firmly on any literary map.

Though today a twenty-first century European city, and with a global reputation, Nottingham has a long and remarkable history. City centre names such as Walnut Tree Lane and Castle Gate, and the Ropewalk for example, evoke memories of a colourful past. Like so many big cities, much has gone, removed because of dire poverty and squalor like the Old Farmhouse in Narrow Marsh which went in 1920, or else buried in the rush to modernisation in the mid-twentieth century. The Victoria bus station was opened in 1972, Broad Marsh shopping centre the same year, and the Victoria shopping centre in 1975. However, in Nottingham, enough remains to give a strong feel of the medieval, and certainly of the eighteenth and nineteenth century town; and long may this continue. The city became a unitary authority in 1998, by 2004 gained a new tramway system which recently expanded, and now has a population of just over 300,000 people.

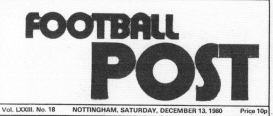

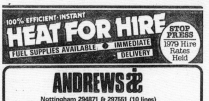

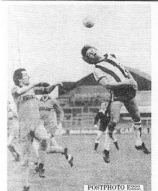

FOOTBALL POST

Vol. LXXIII. No. 18   NOTTINGHAM, SATURDAY, DECEMBER 13, 1980   Price 10p

100% EFFICIENT·INSTANT
HEAT FOR HIRE
FUEL SUPPLIES AVAILABLE · IMMEDIATE · DELIVERY

STOP PRESS
1979 Hire Rates Held

ANDREWS
Nottingham 294871 & 297551 (10 lines)

MAGPIES ON SLIDE AGAIN

PATCHWORK Notts County headed for their first home defeat of the season when Roger Palmer and Darron McDonough scored two second half goals in the space of seven minutes for relegation-worried Oldham Athletic here this afternoon.

County, underlining the paucity of their resources for promotion hopefuls, never built up a rhythm, though teenager Paul Manns should have given them an interval lead.

Palmer pounced in the 55th minute and debut-maker McDonough after 62 minutes to put Oldham on the

DAVID STAPLETON at Meadow Lane

road to their first away victory.

A sparce crowd was quickly appreciative of a pin-point through-ball by Masson that was handled by Hurst as Manns attempted to control the ball.

NOTTS COUNTY	OLDHAM
Avramovic	Platt
Benjamin	Sinclair
O'Brien	Blair
Doherty	Keegan
Kilcline	Clements
Richards	Hurst
Manns	Wylde
Masson	Futcher
Harkouk	Steel
Hunt	Palmer
Wood	McDonough
Sub: Beavon	Sub: Hoolickin

Referee: D. W. Lloyd, Worcester
Linesmen T. J. Holbrook, red flag; R. C. Jackson, yellow flag.

Masson's free-kick was headed clear at his lei-

Your TV matches

ATV
Coventry v WBA

YORKSHIRE
Leeds v Forest

BBC
Aston Villa v Birmingham
Colchester v Yeovil
Swansea v Newcastle

Harkouk did well in an assertive run along the right and the cross into the goalmouth was a good one. But it was cleared

POSTPHOTO E222.

HIGH-FLYING David Hunt stretches to get in a header for Notts County, watched by Oldham's Ronnie Blair, at Meadow Lane this afternoon.

Above: Notts County in the Saturday 13 December 1980 edition of *Football Post,* priced 10p.

Right: Sheriff Reckless' House in Spaniel Row about 1920s with its historic link to George Fox, founder of the Quaker movement in the 1600s. When Fox was arrested, Mistress Reckless, wife of John Reckless, sometime Sheriff of Nottingham, chanced to be in St Mary's Church at the time of the uproar, and was so impressed with what Fox said that she managed to get him removed from the prison and placed in a sort of honourable captivity in her own house.

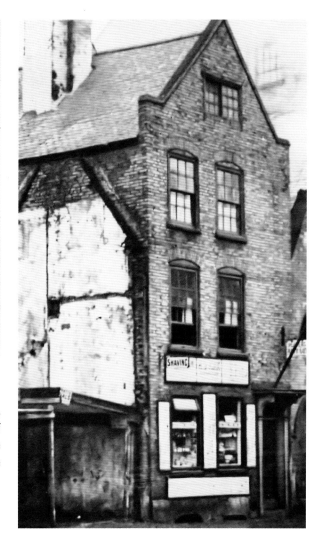

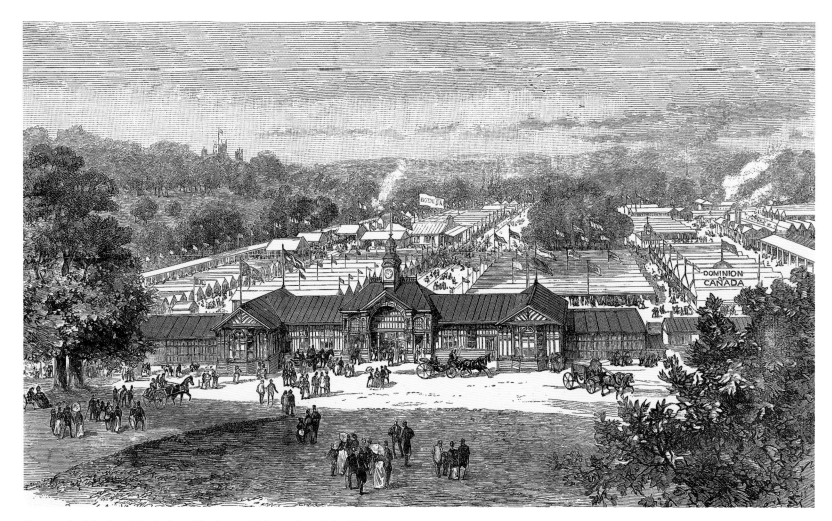

Showyard of the Royal Agricultural Society at Wollaton Park, July 1888.

SOCCER HOMES

The City Ground has been the home of Nottingham Forest since 1898 and has a capacity of 49,000 with seating for 6,450 spectators. The record attendance was set in October 1967 when 49,945 watched the First Division game against Manchester United. The City Ground's playing surface measures 115 yards by 78 yards. Inset: Forest goalkeeper Jim Barron.

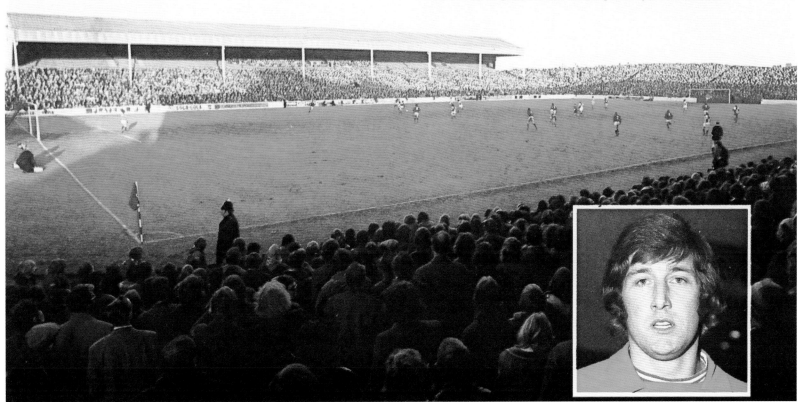

Soccer homes – The City Ground, Nottingham Forest in the 1970s opened in 1898. It had a capacity in the 1970s of 49,945 with only 6,450 seating. Forest have yet to recapture the glory days of Brian Clough. Inset: Goalkeeper Jim Barron.

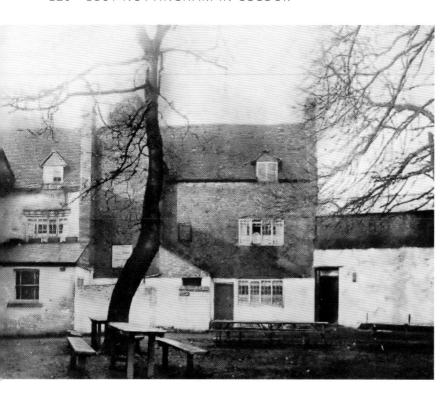

The bowling green at the White Hart Inn at Lenton in the 1920s.

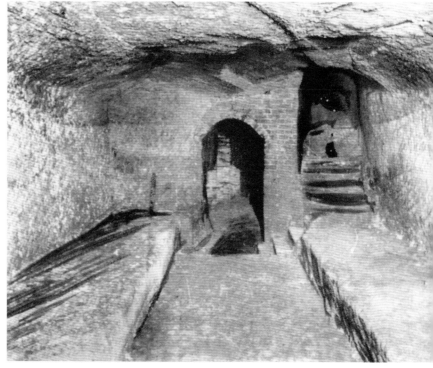

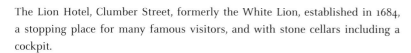

The Lion Hotel, Clumber Street, formerly the White Lion, established in 1684, a stopping place for many famous visitors, and with stone cellars including a cockpit.

The Salutation Inn on Houndsgate and St Nicholas Street or Jew Lane, pictured in the 1920s.

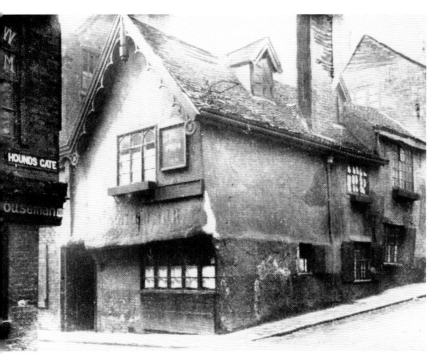

The Theatre Royal in around 1908.

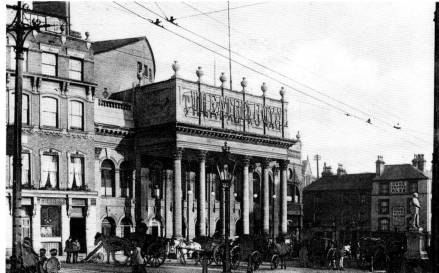

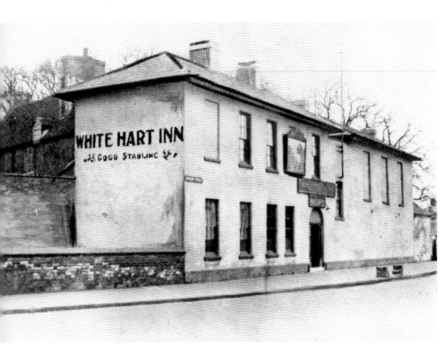

Theatre Square in the 1890s.

The White Hart Inn at Lenton in the 1920s.

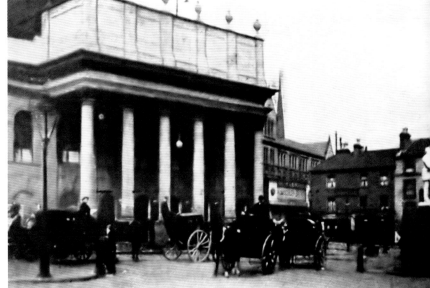

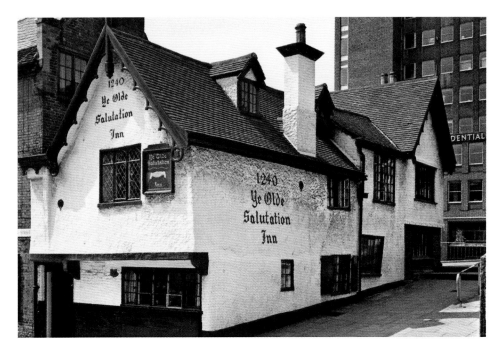

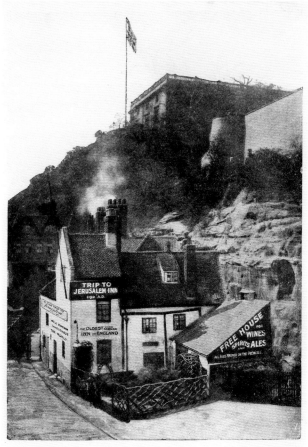

Above: Ye Old Salutation Inn, dating back to 1240.

Right: Ye Olde Trip to Jerusalem Inn, dating from 1189.

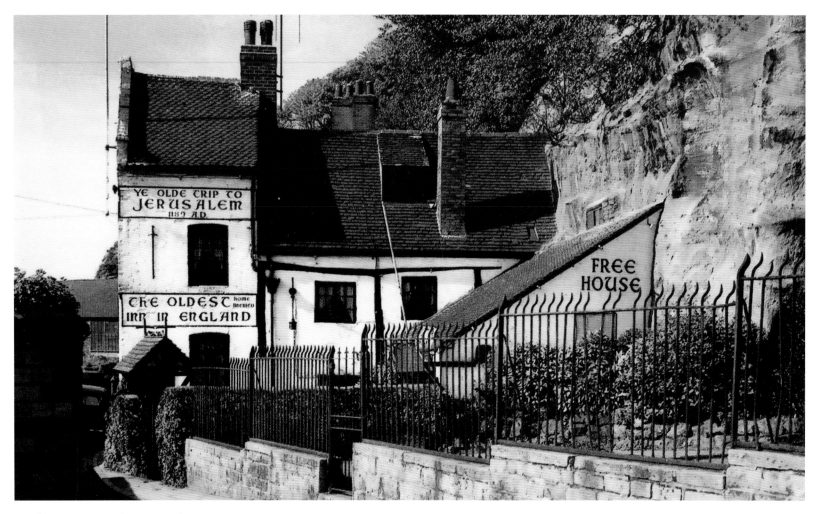

Ye Olde Trip to Jerusalem Inn in the 1980s.

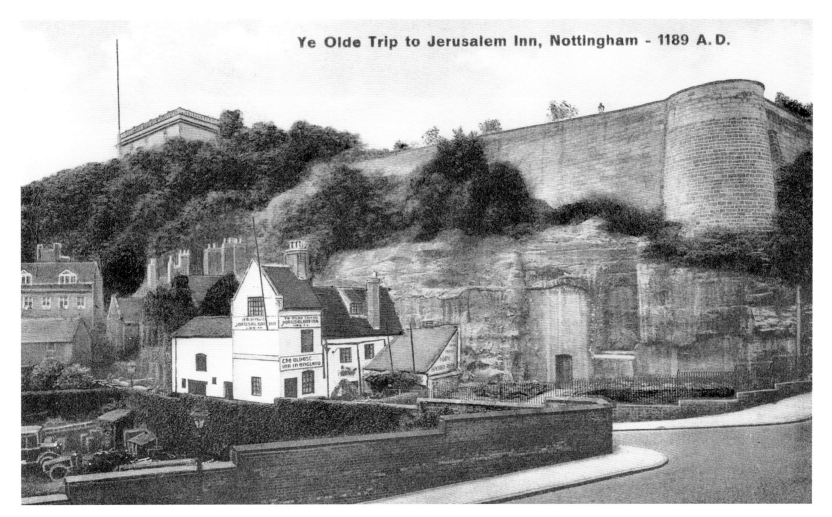

Ye Olde Trip to Jerusalem Inn with the castle behind, from around 1935.

ACKNOWLEDGEMENTS & CREDITS

I thank the series editors and the team at Amberley Publishing for their help, support, and encouragement.

BIBLIOGRAPHY & SUGGESTED READING

There is a wealth of literature on the history of Nottingham, of its people, its heritage, and its industries. These are just a few sources:

Iliffe, R. & Baguley, W. *Victorian Nottingham: A Story in Pictures* (Nottingham Historical Film Unit, 1970).

Jennings, G., *Nottingham and South Notts on Old Postcards: Reflections of a Bygone Age* (Keyworth, 1984).

Kaye, D., *A History of Nottinghamshire* (Phillimore & Co. Ltd, Chichester, 1987).

Mellors, R., *In and About Nottinghamshire. A Book for the Young Men and Women of the City and County* (J. & H. Bell, Nottingham, 1908).

Oldfield, G., *Britain in Old Photographs: Nottingham Past & Present* (Sutton Publishing Limited, Stroud, 1999).

Payne, M., *Britain in Old Photographs: Victorian Nottingham* (Alan Sutton Publishing Limited, Stroud, 1992).

Richards, C., *Nottingham Through Time* (Amberley Publishing, Stroud, 2008).

Rotherham, I. D., *Sherwood Forest & the Dukeries: A Companion to the Land of Robin Hood* (Amberley, Stroud, 2013).

Walker, J. H., *Links with Old Nottingham – Historical Notes* (Nottingham Evening News, 1928).

Walker, J., 'The Alan Sillitoe Interview,' *LeftLion Magazine*, (Nottingham, 2008).

Weir, C. *The Nottinghamshire Heritage* (Phillimore & Co. Ltd, Chichester, 1991).

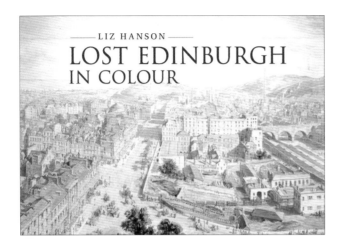
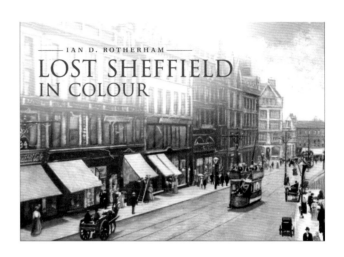